Praise for

Little Faith, Big God

"Have you ever worried that God is displeased with your lack of faith? Feared that you have fallen short in your walk with him? Debbie Wilson answers these questions and more in *Little Faith, Big God*. This thought-provoking, informative, and entertaining book will bring you deeper into your relationship with God. You will never think about faith in the same way again!"

> —**Julie Zine Coleman,** managing editor for Arise Daily and author of *Unexpected Love*

"Life is hard, and at times, faith can be even harder. Yet, of all God's creations, we are the only ones called to live by faith. In *Little Faith, Big God*, Debbie helps reshape our perspective of the spiritual giants who have gone before us. She reminds us that while some stumbled under the weight of their trials, it didn't ruin their relationship with God. It actually helped refine it! In this new book, Debbie takes us on a wonderful journey through the Bible and reminds us that 'impossible problems are no problem for a big God.'"

> —**Amy Richissin,** development with Turning Point, with Dr. David Jeremiah

"In her delightful book *Little Faith, Big God*, Debbie Wilson shares how God has powerfully used ordinary, imperfect people to achieve his extraordinary plans and purposes! Each story contains nuggets of biblical truth, humor, and encouragement to help us on our faith journey. I highly recommend *Little Faith, Big God*."

> —**Josh McDowell,** Christian apologist and best-selling author of *Evidence That Demands a Verdict*

"We live in very confusing times. Christians are increasingly on the defensive, and our hearts cry out to the Lord when politics and culture clash with our faith. *Little Faith, Big God* contains a wealth of Scripture and encouragement in daily devotion, which are wonderful reminders that our mighty God can be trusted completely with our lives and with our worship."

> —**Diane Passno,** former senior vice president of Focus on the Family

"It's difficult to remember that the biblical saints were no saintlier than you or I. God accomplished his will using real people with real struggles, and, fortunately, perfect performance was not required. Nor is it required for you and me. *Little Faith, Big God* reveals the Word in a way that will deepen your walk with Christ through interactive reflections and exercises that encourage personal application."

—**Deb DeArmond,** writing coach and award-winning author of
Bumper Sticker Be-Attitudes

"*Little Faith, Big God* looks creatively at the age-old faith stories found in Hebrews 11. The insights are fresh, and the daily questions helped me to discover both a deeper understanding of Scripture and the true condition of my own heart. The exercise of digging deep into these truths and learning to apply them will make this a faith-changing book for both long time Jesus followers and those new to the journey."

—**Elizabeth Murphy,** speaker and author of *A Roller Coaster, a Roundabout, and a Road Trip*

"Debbie's at her best as she helps us relate to the examples of faith showcased in Hebrews 11. God turned their flaws into their strengths—and he can do the same to ours. *Little Faith, Big God* reminds us that we're all in process, yet, by his grace, our inadequacies can become our strengths. Want to draw your sense of self-worth and significance from God instead of your performance? Then *Little Faith, Big God* is a must-read."

—**Lisa T. Grimes,** speaker and coauthor of *Remember Who You Are*

"With compassion, depth, and a solid biblical foundation, Debbie Wilson takes the readers through the lives of the heroes of the faith in Hebrews 11. With wisdom and tenderness, she emphasizes obedience and surrender to God's will in order to fulfill our purpose on earth. Wilson's personal stories and application questions help draw readers into a desire to begin strengthening their personal relationships with God. I highly recommend this book."

—**Yvonne Ortega,** licensed professional counselor and author of the
Moving from Broken to Beautiful series

"Faith is a slippery subject for many until they have walked the path of life and find it. Debbie Wilson's book will help those who are searching for answers about faith. She uses Scripture, history, examples, illustrations, and personal testimonies to help us focus on our faith—a great teaching tool. *Little Faith, Big God* is a must-read because 'without faith, it is impossible to please God.'"

—**Donald A. Woeltjen,** South Georgia Conference of the United Methodist Church

"What I truly value about this book is that it makes the gospel seem so simple. And isn't that exactly what God would want for us? As Christians, we have developed ways to create an incredibly complicated message of faith, and yet it's not! *Little Faith, Big God* provides a way for us to take God at his word, with concrete ways to do that. This book is ideal for group studies."

—**Shari Braendel,** author of *Help Me Jesus, I Have Nothing to Wear!*

"*Little Faith, Big God* is so much more than a devotional or Bible study! Debbie invites the reader to travel with her through Scripture as she surveys the faith journeys of some significant men and women. Her probing questions and the myriad of real-life stories she shares bring faith to life and make it relatable to everyone."

—**Craig Phelps,** lead pastor at Gorman Baptist Church, Durham, North Carolina

"In *Little Faith, Big God*, Debbie has a rare ability to bring to life people of old in a way that is relevant to today. You'll be inspired to apply life lessons from these very real people who made a forever impact in their generation and beyond. This book will deepen your love and appreciation for Jesus and will help grow your faith in our very big God!"

—**Tara Furman,** founder and president of Knowing God Ministries

"As I read *Little Faith Big God*, I realized this is every person's story. We are weak, but he is strong. Our faith is little, but God is big. This story brings rest to your soul and peace to your heart. This journey is not about perfect performance but trusting a big God who loves all people—even those of us with little faith."

—**Monica Schmelter,** host of *Bridges* on Christian Television Network

"Debbie Wilson walks us through the personal struggles of those named in Hebrews 11 in a way that helps us connect with them and re-energizes our trust in God because we know how their lives worked out for good.

Even though we do not know the ends of our stories, we can trust that God's grace is in the details of our lives and that he never gives up. *Little Faith, Big God* will continue to linger in your mind, heart, and soul."

—**Annetta Dellinger,** author of *Joy-spirations for Caregivers* and *Blessings and Prayers for Those with Cancer*

"We live by faith and not by sight. But what exactly does that mean? And how do we do that? Debbie offers clear steps not only to grow our faith but also to have the vibrant life God intended, one full of grace. My heart was blessed by *Little Faith, Big God*, and I trust yours will be too."

—**Diane Rumley,** cofounder and executive director of Support Military Families

Little Faith
Big God

Little Faith Big God

GRACE TO GROW

WHEN YOUR FAITH

FEELS SMALL

Debbie W. Wilson

LEAFWOOD
PUBLISHERS

an imprint of Abilene Christian University Press

LITTLE FAITH, BIG GOD

Grace to Grow When Your Faith Feels Small

LEAFWOOD
P U B L I S H E R S
an imprint of Abilene Christian University Press

Copyright © 2020 by Debbie W. Wilson

ISBN 978-1-68426-430-8 | LCCN 2019038043

Printed in the United States of America

LIBRARY OF CONGRESS CATALOGING-IN-PUBLICATION DATA
Names: Wilson, Debbie W, 1952- author.
Title: Little faith, big God : grace to grow when your faith feels small /
    Debbie W Wilson.
Description: Abilene : Leafwood Publishers, 2020. | Includes
    bibliographical references.
Identifiers: LCCN 2019038043 | ISBN 9781684264308 (paperback)
Subjects: LCSH: Bible. Hebrews, XI—Textbooks. | Bible. Hebrews,
    XI—Criticism, interpretation, etc. | Faith—Biblical teaching.
Classification: LCC BS2775.55 .W55 2020 | DDC 227/.870071—dc23
LC record available at https://lccn.loc.gov/2019038043

Cover design by Thinkpen Design | Interior text design by Sandy Armstrong, Strong Design

Leafwood Publishers is an imprint of Abilene Christian University Press

ACU Box 29138, Abilene, Texas 79699

1–877–816–4455 | www.leafwoodpublishers.com

20 21 22 23 24 25 / 7 6 5 4 3 2 1

To Larry Wilson, my husband, life partner, and best friend. Your love for the Lord captivated me the first time I saw you. Thank you for loving me well and enriching my life with your depth, laughter, and encouragement.

To Susie Browne, my friend and partner in ministry and prayer. Your steadfast faith, hope, and love in the midst of adversity bolster my faith when it feels small.

And to you, dear reader, may the Lord enrich you as you walk in his grace.

Table of Contents

Acknowledgments

This book wouldn't be here without the prayers and encouragement of God's people.

Thank you, Lisa Grimes, for asking me to lead a study at your house for your neighbors—if they'd come. Not only did they come, but they also invited their friends! Your friendship and support are invaluable. You are the friend everyone wants.

Thank you to my special intercessors and prayer partners: Susie Browne, Nan Sawaia, and Yvonne Ortega. Your prayers put wind in my sails.

I thank God for our Thursday morning group of Jesus Girls who participated in this study as it was being shaped and who enrich my life weekly.

A special thanks to my Leafwood Publishers team: Jason Fikes, Duane Anderson, Rebecka Scott, Caleb Gravitt, and those I don't know by name. You are a delight to work with.

I also want to thank my husband, Larry Wilson, and daughter, Ginny Wilson, for their encouragement, and a special thank you to Ginny and her Bible study for going through the material in the early stages.

Most of all, my deepest gratitude goes to our Lord Jesus, our big God who carries me by his grace.

Welcome and Introduction

I USED TO BE ADDICTED TO PERFORMANCE. AND DARK CHOColate. Now I'm *mostly* addicted to chocolate.

When my husband, Larry, said, "You sure are hard on yourself," I recognized the remnants of my unhealthy tendency to draw significance from how well I think I've performed. So many of us tend to base our worth on what we do instead of who we are in Christ. How can we stop this destructive cycle? What does God expect of his children?

I find strength in the stories of the believers named in Hebrews 11. Where I see flaws, God saw magnificent faith. These imperfect men and women pleased God. That challenges and encourages me. Challenges, because we don't get a pass because we're flawed. Encourages, because God uses inadequate people.

God calls us his children. And children make messes they can't clean up. They need to be trained, loved, and nurtured. We anticipate that. As a boy, even Jesus "grew in wisdom and stature, and in favor with God and man" (Luke 2:52). If God expects growth to be a process, shouldn't we?

Spiritual health is not instant, but neither is it stagnant. Vibrant faith grows stronger with proper use. The heroes whose stumbles reassured me also inspired me with their dynamic faith.

In his book *Leadership in the Nineties*, Dr. J. Robert Clinton suggests that at least 70 percent of leaders do not finish well. They often fail to listen and keep growing, and eventually lose their convictions along the way. When a friend shared this startling observation with me, I thought of the people we'll soon visit in Hebrews 11, the "faith chapter" of the Bible. Despite their weaknesses, they finished well and earned God's approval.

Like children who beam at their parent's praise, I think every true believer longs to hear "Well done, my good and faithful servant" at the end of his or her life. I know I do. That healthy desire propels me to persevere in faith when I'm tempted to retreat in fear. Yet if we aren't careful, that longing can produce striving that puts the focus on us instead of on God. Perhaps this is why so many leaders burn out.

What set the men and women in Hebrews 11 apart? What can they teach us about God-pleasing faith and how to bounce back from failure? Hebrews 13:7 says, "Consider the outcome of their way of life and imitate their faith." Together, let's consider these individuals "whose weakness was turned to strength" and find the specific aspects of their faith that we can imitate.

If you've wondered how God feels about you when you falter, if the weight of unexpected bills or strained relationships threatens to sink your spirit, or if your three steps forward seem to be followed by two back, then allow the faithful witnesses of Hebrews 11 to equip and encourage you. Faith stories are grace stories. God's grace fuels our stories too!

The Layout

For convenience, each chapter is divided into five daily lessons. Of course, you can review these at your own speed. The questions contained throughout are designed to stimulate your thinking about a particular Scripture passage and help you consider personal applications. Feel free to ask your own questions. Becoming a biblical thinker and able listener of God creates a solid foundation for your faith.

To get the most from your time, you will need a Bible. I suggest you have one you are free to underline or highlight. For your convenience, Hebrews 11 is printed out for you at the end of this book. You may also enjoy listening to the Scripture readings being read aloud on an audio Bible app in a familiar version, a modern idiomatic translation like *The Message*, or a dramatic reading. Sometimes, I listen to an audio version of the Bible while driving, chopping vegetables, or getting in my walking steps. Listening to Scripture helps me hear things I may not have noticed when reading the same passage in my Bible. I also suggest that you begin each lesson by asking the Lord to speak to you personally.

In your personal time, be completely open with the Lord and yourself. If you go through this material with a group or a friend, you need only contribute what you are comfortable sharing with others. I learn so much from other people's questions and observations, and I encourage you to find a group that welcomes discussion.

My prayer is that hungry hearts will discover the understanding they need to live by faith and finish well. Let's pray.

Lord Jesus, thank you for inviting us to live each day with you. Grant us ears to hear, eyes to see, and hearts to receive all you have for us. In Jesus's name. Amen!

Becoming What God Sees in You

You Can Live by Faith

"For we live by faith, not by sight."
—2 Corinthians 5:7

BEFORE I WAS EVEN OUT OF MY DRIVEWAY, THE GPS APP ON my phone said I'd arrive five minutes late. *Groan.* I was on my way to a group that had invited me to visit after discussing one of my books. My cheeks burned at the thought of walking in late.

Why can't you leave on time? What's wrong with you? My thoughts chided me.

This line of thinking neither helped me make up for lost time nor prepared my heart to encourage the women I'd see. I thought of a novel I'd recently finished with an imperfect heroine. If she ran late, I empathized with her. So why was I so hard on myself?

I shifted my thoughts off myself and on to God. I thanked him for making me who I am. I asked him to help me with my weakness, to work this situation out for good—and to help me arrive on time!

A woman pulled in behind me as I parked my car. She jumped out of her car and raced to open the door. "I was so glad to see you drive up. If I walk in with the speaker, I'm not late." We both laughed.

God used my timing, or my lack thereof, to build a bond. I entered relaxed and happy to be there. Would that have happened if I'd stayed self-absorbed, brooding over my weaknesses?

Reading how God dealt with his flawed children in Hebrews 11 has helped me give myself grace when I mess up. God gave Jacob a spectacular dream in which the Lord stood at the top of a ladder that spanned the gap between heaven and earth, with angels ascending and descending it.

God blessed Jacob in the dream and promised to give him and his descendants the land of Canaan. He was bequeathing the promise of Abraham. What amazed me about this scene is its *timing*. Jacob had just deceived his father and cheated his brother Esau.

God showed similar grace to Abraham, who lied about the nature of his relationship with Sarah, and to Samson, with all of his moral failures. If God is patient with his children, shouldn't we emulate him and extend grace to ourselves as well? Living in regret doesn't move us forward. But if we surrender our flaws and flops to God, he will use them for his glory and our good.

Perhaps the key to accepting ourselves—which precedes the ability to unconditionally love others—comes from seeing ourselves as our Lord sees us. "Even before he made the world, God loved us and chose us in Christ to be holy and without fault in his eyes" (Eph. 1:4 NLT). When he looks at us, he sees what we will be.

The ancients of Hebrews 11 confirm the hope of this truth. "And having chosen them, he called them to come to him. And having called them, he gave them right standing with himself. And having given them right standing, he gave them his glory" (Rom. 8:30 NLT). This week, we meet the heroes of Hebrews 11 and see what made them commendable.

Day One

Faith in the Unseen

"We don't serve apostates," Caleb spit the words at Miriam.

"Cousin, I worship God. I didn't quit being Jewish when I found the Messiah."

"Out," he pointed. "Or do you want me to throw you out?"

Miriam dropped the bag of grain. If Caleb thought he'd see her cry, he was wrong. She wouldn't cry—at least not until she was out of view. Jesus, where are you? We're starving. Have you forgotten us?

Persecution rained down on the early church (Heb. 10:32–34). Under Nero, martyrdom became part of the Christian experience for those in Rome. Many theologians believe the book of Hebrews was written for Jewish believers who were considering returning to Judaism to escape the hardships that Christianity brought them.

These Hebrew Christians had already suffered much for their faith in Christ. Hebrews 12:4 says, "you have not yet resisted to the point of shedding your blood." This raises the possibility that the persecution of these believers was becoming more intense.

These suffering saints needed hope. They needed to remember the superiority of Christ over the old covenant and be reminded that God still speaks today. Hebrews 11 supplied them with a definition of faith and examples of those who had finished well, in order to sustain them through their own trials.

We too need hope. The world is a hostile place for Christ-followers (John 15:18–21). Just as the serpent slid into Eden and seduced Eve with his lies, predators slip into our homes through cyberspace and snatch the hearts of those we love. Schools mock Christian viewpoints. Workplaces indoctrinate believers to replace biblical love with political correctness. And people we love misunderstand our devotion to Christ.

In addition, we have a spiritual foe who browbeats us with doubts and fears. Shallow confidence collapses under such opposition. But hungry hearts dig deeper to uncover a faith overflowing with hope. Little faith in a big God blossoms into courage to sustain us through every trial and setback.

Before we explore the individual players in this chapter, let's take an overview of the first half of Hebrews chapter 11. Jesus commends childlike faith. Approach the Bible with childlike wonder and ask the Holy Spirit to reveal truth. As you read today's passage, notice the role that *faith* plays.

Scripture Reading..

HEBREWS 11:1–12

Study and Reflection

Faith = confidence + assurance

1. What stood out from today's reading?

   #3 what was <del>not</del> seen was not made from that which is visible

2. What lessons and personal applications do you take from this passage? *patient, perseverance, trust.*

   Faith

3. What do you learn about faith? — *our Faith pleases God.*

   (Faith brings Hope) you may not see what you are looking for / time will tell

4. Did this passage raise any questions you hope to have answered in this study? *more*

   what are the practical steps? The Building Blocks to faith?

Faith in Our Creator

We practice what we believe. Before listing what people of faith *did*, Hebrews chapter 11 says what people of faith *know*. "By faith we understand that the entire universe was formed at God's command, that what we now see did not come from anything that can be seen" (Heb. 11:3 NLT).

Believing God created the world puts us in the company of those commended for their faith and impacts the quality of our relationship with God.

Every creation begins with an idea. Even the chair I'm sitting on existed in a designer's head before it supported my weight. Whereas a craftsman used wood and fabric to turn an idea into a chair, God spoke fragrant forests, twinkling stars, and prickly porcupines into being. If humans use wood to bring their ideas into existence, is it too much to believe God used words to create his designs?

Although it takes faith to understand that God formed the universe by simply speaking, the visible world points to a creator. No one stumbles upon a cabin in the woods, smells bacon wafting from an open window, and doubts human involvement. The miracle of birth, of daffodils bursting forth after the dead of winter, of an eagle teaching her young to fly all reveal intelligent design.

> What may be known about God is plain to them,
> because God has made it plain to them. For since the
> creation of the world God's invisible qualities—his eter-
> nal power and divine nature—have been clearly seen,
> being understood from what has been made, so that
> people are without excuse. (Rom. 1:19–20)

If we doubt God created the world, then what hope do we have that he can handle our trials? How can we trust his promises if the Bible got this wrong? But, if he made the universe by speaking, then nothing is too difficult for him.

The ancients believed in the Creator. The prophet Jeremiah wrote, "Ah Lord God! Behold, You have made the heavens and the earth by Your great power and by Your outstretched arm! Nothing is too difficult for You" (Jer. 32:17 NASB).

No matter where they were dispersed, creation reminded them that God was near. Knowing Jesus is one with the Creator and not new to God's story provides another anchor to our faith (Col. 1:15–17; Heb. 1:1–3).

When we can't fathom how our prayers will be answered, creation whispers, "Remember your Creator."

CLOSING PRAYER

Use this space to turn your insights and responses into a personal prayer. Thank God for the ways he's revealed himself through nature. Ask him to open your eyes to his signature on creation.

I Want to Remember . . .

What do you want to remember from today's study? Let's encourage each other by sharing our takeaways on social media with the hashtag #LittleFaithBigGod.

Day Two
Faith in God's Timing

After a hairdresser scalped me a couple of hours before I was to stand and speak before a few hundred women, I now willingly pay double for someone I trust. Faith in God is much like trust in a good hairdresser. We trust him with what we do not see because of what we already know. Ruth M. Bathauer writes that faith "is not trust in the *unknown* but rather in the *unseen*."[1]

The One who painted the wings of butterflies will, at the appointed time, fulfill every promise. But as we'll see, some of God's spectacular promises won't be realized until the final chapter of his story. God is bigger than a lifespan.

We view life like someone standing on a sidewalk watching a parade pass by. We see only what passes in front of us. God sees the story of humankind as one looking down on the parade from a blimp. He sees the beginning, middle, and end all at the same time. His ways are always better than ours. He has information that we lack. It makes good sense to trust him. Although biblical faith relates to the unseen, it isn't blind.

As you read today's passage, continue to notice references to *faith* and repeated ideas.

Scripture Reading...
HEBREWS 11:13–22, 39–40

Study and Reflection

1. Write your observations from today's reading.

    We may not receive the Blessings in our lifetime. For the goal of the community / world

2. What lessons and personal applications can you glean?

    Faith => for the good of a great world / community

3. All these people were still living by faith—not in doubt or disappointment—when they died.

    ✱ accept what we are getting / not waiting !!!

25

a. Considering "They did not receive the things promised" (see verses 13 and 39), what makes their faith remarkable?

obedient / Faithful / patient

b. What do you learn about God's timetable?

Long, unpredictable.

c. How do you reconcile this with the following promise: "For the Scripture says, 'WHOEVER BELIEVES IN HIM WILL NOT BE DISAPPOINTED'" (Rom. 10:11 NASB).

We will receive other blessings.
To replace disappointment? / This life is not the only one

Welcomed from a Distance

People of faith keep an eternal perspective. They know the plans of an everlasting God stretch further than a human lifetime.

From a distance, the patriarchs saw the fulfillment of God's promises, not with physical eyes but through eyes of faith. God's daily care and company were enough for this life. He would fulfill his promise in the future, and they would see it.

Biblical faith is not a leap in the dark. The invisible answers to your faith-born prayers will one day be as palpable as the ocean's crashing waves and sand between your toes. The actions of the men and women in Hebrews showed they believed God's promises. We join their company when we believe what God says.

CLOSING PRAYER

Use this space to turn your insights and responses into prayers.

Visualize God's promise, something not yet seen, yet will happen.
Dale being more of a loving Husb

I Want to Remember . . .

Today's takeaways from #LittleFaithBigGod are: *one foot in front of the other, pray, Be thankful, look to God's creation to renew faith.*

Day Three

— *Don't be disappointed!*

Faith in God's Character

What does faith look like? A woman I once knew thought faith was rubbing the arthritic joints in her hands and claiming they were getting better. She repeated this every day. Is that what the Bible means when it says, "faith is the assurance of things hoped for, the conviction of things not seen" (Heb. 11:1 NASB)?

Bible commentator Dr. R. Kent Hughes wrote, "To do a thing 'by faith' you must do it in response to and according to a word from God. You hear God's word indicating his will, and 'by faith' you respond in obedience. 'Faith comes by hearing, and hearing through the word of Christ' (Rom. 10:17)."[2]

Hebrews 11 uses real people to show us faith in action. Some of them cause us to scratch our heads because their flaws stand out more than their faith. Yet Hebrews 11 remembers their faith.

Since "we all stumble in many ways" (James 3:2), I'm thankful God included the rest of their stories in other Scriptures. Their inconsistent lives remind us that the nearness of God, not a blameless performance, is our good (Ps. 73:22–23). His strong grip keeps us safe when we fall.

What Is Faith?

Faith is taking God at his word. For Abel, it meant coming to God the way he'd provided. For Abraham, it was advancing in the hope he'd produce an heir while his body deteriorated before his very eyes.

How I apply faith may change with life's seasons. It may mean staying home with small children when I feel more comfortable in a boardroom. It may mean taking on a challenge when I'd rather cling to my comfort. It is as individual as we are. But faith has some common threads. Let's look at how God defines faith and hope.

Scripture Reading..
HEBREWS 11:1–6

Study and Reflection

1. Use Hebrews 11:1 and 6 to describe biblical faith in your own words. "Now faith is the assurance of things hoped for, the conviction of things not seen. . . . And without faith it is impossible to please Him, for he who comes to God must believe that He is and that He is a rewarder of those who seek Him" (Heb. 11:1, 6 NASB). *You must believe God who is unseen, a conviction (by creation) that he is the creator. and to seek him.*

2. We often use the term *hope* for wishful thinking. We hope for something that's uncertain. Biblical hope refers to a confident assertion. Faith in a good, powerful, and perfect God is the foundation for unwavering hope. How did these people find hope when they felt discouraged and couldn't change their circumstances? *World is fallen, look to God who is good.*

    a. "Why, my soul, are you downcast? Why so disturbed within me? Put your hope in God, for I will yet praise him, my Savior and my God" (Ps. 42:11).

b. "The thought of my suffering and homelessness is bitter beyond words. I will never forget this awful time, as I grieve over my loss. Yet I still dare to hope when I remember this: The faithful love of the LORD never ends! His mercies never cease. Great is his faithfulness; his mercies begin afresh each morning. I say to myself, 'The LORD is my inheritance; therefore, I will hope in him!'" (Lam. 3:19–24 NLT).

put worth in godly things. Faith will all fall away.

3. How is placing our hope in Jesus different from putting our hope in a specific outcome (for example, getting the job position we want)? *Getting that Job may not be God's plan.*

4. Hebrews 11:1 and 6 refer to things unseen by us. Why does relying on <u>physical</u> sight for understanding hinder us?

a. "So we fix our eyes not on what is seen, but on what is unseen, since what is seen is temporary, but what is unseen is eternal" (2 Cor. 4:18). *What we see is of the world + will pass away.*

world + lies

b. "Trust in the LORD with all your heart and lean not on your own understanding; in all your ways submit to him, and he will make your paths straight" (Prov. 3:5–6). *Lessen anxiety! we don't know what we don't know*

c. "Then Jesus told him, 'Because you have seen me, you have believed; blessed are those who have not seen and yet have believed'" (John 20:29). *Don't always strive to see things. Have faith.*

d. "When the servant of the man of God got up early the next morning and went outside, there were troops, horses, and chariots everywhere. 'Oh, sir, what will we do now?' the young man cried to Elisha.

'Don't be afraid!' Elisha told him. 'For there are more on our side than on theirs!' Then Elisha prayed, 'O Lord, open his eyes and let him see!' The Lord opened the young man's eyes, and when he looked up, he saw that the hillside around Elisha was filled with horses and chariots of fire" (2 Kings 6:15–17 NLT).

5. From the following, what role does trust in God play in our ability to experience hope? "May the God of hope fill you with all joy and peace as you trust in him, so that you may overflow with hope by the power of the Holy Spirit" (Rom. 15:13). *Trust in God, trust in the unseen, put our weight in God.*

What Gives You Hope?

Placing our hope in God instead of in a particular outcome has practical ramifications, especially when what we hope for may not happen. I experienced this the night before I was to fly standby to a vacation reservation.

Because our daughter works for an airline, we can fly standby at a reduced rate when seats are available. In the day of overbooked flights, that often means flying on a prayer. A planned vacation to Yosemite National Park for my husband's birthday was no exception.

We scheduled our trip around the flight loads. Since the park was filling up, we had to book nonrefundable accommodations ahead of time.

The night before our departure, we learned that all the flights out of Raleigh for the next couple of days were overbooked. I loathed the thought of getting up before dawn and sitting at the airport for nothing. I also hated to pay for reservations we wouldn't be able to use.

We packed, hoping two seats would miraculously open up. In the meantime, I reminded myself that God was greater than this situation. We'd prayed as we planned our trip. God knew about this when we'd booked our lodging. Maybe someone else needed our cabin. I asked for grace to trust and not grumble, no matter what happened.

At 2:00 a.m. our bedroom door opened. "Mom, you don't need to get up before 7. I found you seats on another airline," my daughter whispered.

Wonderful! The next day I learned just how astonishing this was.

The Evidence of Things Not Seen

Our half-empty plane puzzled Larry and me. How could there be so many empty seats Tuesday morning when there had been no seats Monday night?

While making our connecting flight in Phoenix, I learned the reason. Late the previous night, a plane's air conditioning had broken. The airline had successfully rerouted most of their passengers. Shortly after midnight, they added an extra plane—our plane—to accommodate the remaining travelers. I told my daughter, Ginny, what had happened, and she told me the rest of the story.

At 1:45 a.m. that morning, Ginny had felt an undeniable prompting to call a specific carrier. She resisted. She works in reservations and knew airlines always list their flights on the computer. Why the urge to phone? Finally, she obeyed the unseen guide. The person who took her call stunned her by having available seats.

Maybe the flight was not listed because it was a last-minute, one-time-only flight. All I know is that when a seasoned airline employee couldn't find seats, God created some and directed her to them!

The Assurance of Hoped-For Things

Not all situations turn out as we hope. An ice storm kept me from using confirmed seats to a conference. Even then, faith calmed my fretting by reminding me that God's will for my life is perfect (Rom. 12:2). I didn't fly off for my conference, but I didn't fly off the handle either. As C. S. Lewis's Narnian Marsh-Wiggle consoled the children in *The Silver Chair* when their obedience seemed to have led to a dangerous dead end: "'Don't you mind,' said Puddleglum. 'There *are* no accidents. Our guide is Aslan; and he was there when the giant king caused the letters to be cut, and he knew already all things that would come of them; including *this.*'"[3]

I missed one day of the conference, but our family enjoyed huddling around the fireplace amid the snow and ice. And God provided a seat on a flight the following morning. Faith allowed me to fly higher and enjoy a situation I could not change instead of brooding over it.

Our hope rests in a loving God. Even though we can't see his invisible hand or understand his plan, like the wind, his goodness is evident to those with eyes of faith.

When stormy emotions cloud your spiritual vision, focus on your Pilot. Then choose to trust him with your groundings.

CLOSING PRAYER

Do you wrestle over something you can't understand? Have your "whys" pushed God away? Why not bring your confusion to him? Tell him about your disappointment. Then surrender your need to understand. Thank him that he never makes a mistake and choose to trust him by faith. Take the time you need to make peace with God today. Ask him to help you trust him more.

I Want to Remember . . .

Today's takeaways from #LittleFaithBigGod are:

[handwritten notes: Hope for things unseen / Faith is / Prove that / Look ahead / Calm / Joyful submission]

Day Four
Faith in the Right Model

My friend Rhonda Rhea says, "If a wolf ever puts on a nightgown, and I can't tell he's not my grandma, I think that means I'm not visiting my grandma nearly often enough." That seems so obvious, and yet how many of us have been duped by wolves in familiar clothing?

We once had a pastor who turned out to be a wolf in shepherd's clothing. Like a conjuring artist, his dynamic preaching diverted his congregants' attention away from his covert attacks on the faithful. His deceit eventually became obvious, and many left not only his flock but, sadly, they quit attending any church.

Those of us who have been wounded by people we've respected in the church may be wary of looking at human examples of faith. Jesus and the writers of the New Testament warned against wolves that would slip into the sheepfold dressed as sheep. And wolves aren't the only ones that cause harm. Immature and worldly believers also injure fellow sheep (1 Cor. 3:1–3).

Paul told the church to imitate him *as he imitated Christ Jesus.* There is only one perfect example of faith—Jesus. We must not let a bad experience with religion or the religious distract us from knowing and loving him.

Hebrews 12:2 reminds us to fix "our eyes on Jesus, the author and perfecter of faith." Jesus perfectly modeled how to walk with God during his days on earth. Biblical faith is rooted in him. Trusting anything less—bank accounts, politics, and people—provides as much security as trusting someone just because she's called "Grandma." Bank accounts can be depleted. Politics fluctuate like Oklahoma weather. People leave and die. But Jesus never changes.

Scripture Reading..
Hebrews 12:1–3

Study and Reflection

1. What makes Jesus worthy of our trust? "In the past God spoke to our ancestors through the prophets at many times and in various ways, but in these last days he has spoken to us by his Son, whom he appointed heir of all things, and through whom also he made the universe. The Son is the radiance of God's glory and the exact representation of his being, sustaining all things by his powerful word" (Heb. 1:1–3).

   Sent by God, worthy of our trust, perfect example.

2. What would it look like for you to follow Jesus's example in the following verses?

   a. "I seek not to please myself but him who sent me" (John 5:30).

   major change of course. In some areas

b. "So Jesus said, '. . . I do nothing on my own but speak just what the Father has taught me'" (John 8:28).

I need to change my attitude and actions toward Dale, I'm bitter. Need gentleness, kindness

3. From our human perspective, God's ways may appear counterproductive and even foolish. It doesn't make sense to allow missionaries to be martyred or mothers of young children to die of cancer. Besides the problem of our limited understanding, wounds and critical authority figures from childhood create obstacles to trusting God. What do you learn from the following that could help you build trust in God? Personalize your answers.

a. "And do not be conformed to this world, but be transformed by the renewing of your mind, so that you may prove what the will of God is, that which is good and acceptable and perfect" (Rom. 12:2 NASB). *This world would say confront Dale, call her out on this B.S. – how can I do that?*

b. "'For I know the plans I have for you,' declares the LORD, 'plans to prosper you and not to harm you, plans to give you hope and a future'" (Jer. 29:11).

mysterious ways

c. "As the heavens are higher than the earth, so are my ways higher than your ways and my thoughts than your thoughts" (Isa. 55:9).

pray higher, higher perspective!

d. "For the foolishness of God is wiser than human wisdom, and the weakness of God is stronger than human strength" (1 Cor. 1:25). *I can relate to this!*

e. "Take my yoke upon you and learn from me, for I am gentle and humble in heart, and you will find rest for your souls" (Matt. 11:29). *Heartening.*

True wisdom.

4. The Apostle Paul wrote, "I know whom I have believed" (2 Tim. 1:12). Consider an area where you currently feel unsettled. In whom or what are you trusting?

I'm trusting my own judgment & it's not working!

5. How is faith different from wishing?

Faith - godly control. *faith is more like waiting/patiently*

Dealing with Pesky Doubts about God's Goodness ✱

"Do you give samples of your chicken salad?" my friend asked our server.

"No ma'am," he replied, leaving us to ponder our menus.

"I guess I'll order something else," she said.

As we enjoyed our meal, the manager dropped by our table to ask how our food was. We told her it was great. Then my friend repeated her question.

"We aren't able to offer samples because we make each dish fresh when it's ordered," she said.

Her answer provided a legitimate reason for why they wouldn't offer samples. But I still wasn't convinced. I couldn't imagine them chopping celery and nuts for one serving of chicken salad at a time.

When I arrived home, I received an email from my friend, who frequents the restaurant we'd just left. She'd remembered that their chicken salad was not the prepared dish we'd pictured, but a green salad with a grilled chicken breast on top. I laughed at our misunderstanding.

Chicken Salad and the Bible

I know God's ways are perfect. But sometimes they don't look that way. I've wrestled through some Old Testament laws and the book of Job. Add to this the suffering I see around me. While I choose to trust him, some pesky questions still bother me. One day, I asked God:

- Why would you allow Job to suffer so much loss, pain, and misunderstanding when you said no one was as righteous as Job?
- Why did you treat slaves differently than free people and women differently than men?
- Why do you allow unrighteous judges to take away the rights of the innocent to protect the wicked?
- Why do you allow a faithful believer to suffer on a deathbed of pain and the wicked to die peacefully in their sleep?

God addressed my questions and then used the chicken salad incident to quiet my lingering doubts. I realized that if a restaurant manager had good reasons for what first appeared to be arbitrary rules, then my wise Father also has good reasons for how he runs the world.

God is like the ocean; I'm like a child trying to understand the mysteries of the deep from my small pail of water. I can't understand someone so much greater than I am. But I can trust that he is wiser and more loving than I can imagine.

can't see the forest for the trees

Job got the opportunity to bring his questions to God. Instead of explaining the background of Job's circumstances and his good intentions for Job, God asked Job to explain the mysteries of the seen world.

If Job couldn't explain the mysteries of creation, how could he hope to understand the mysteries of the Creator? Job's questions evaporated in that tiny glimpse of God's majesty.

I used to say that some questions wouldn't be answered until we get to heaven. Now I think that when I see the Lord, my questions will no longer matter.

Faith in a Person

Biblical faith rests on the character of God. Jesus came to show us the Father. The better we know him, the less our questions bother us.

One key characteristic sets people with commendable faith apart. They trust God's character and align their behavior with his revealed will.

If we focus on the size of our faith, we're in danger of becoming either paralyzed by our inadequacy or proud and self-reliant. We aren't enough for life's challenges (2 Cor. 3:5). Jesus is the object of genuine faith. And he's always enough.

CLOSING PRAYER

Use this space to turn your insights and responses into prayers. Ask the Holy Spirit to teach you the truth about the character of Jesus and the Father.

That is a good step.

I Want to Remember . . .

Today's takeaways from #LittleFaithBigGod are:

Day Five

Faith in God's Word

Does our view of the origin of life really matter? The church youth group I attended growing up viewed the Genesis account of creation as an allegory. When I started reading the Bible, I found that perspective collided with the New Testament. Both the apostles and Jesus treated Genesis as a true account. People, not ape-like creatures, made up the first family. Doubting this part of the Bible compromises our faith in other essentials.

Think about it. What hope do those who deny a personal Creator have? How can we trust him with our eternities if we don't believe what he says? Who do we call on in time of need? Who do we thank for a beautiful sunset or good health?

In his book *The Shadow of Forgotten Ancestors: A Search for Who We Are*, cosmic scientist Carl Sagan wrote, "We humans are like a newborn baby left on a doorstep without a note explaining who we are, where we came from, and who our parents might be."[4]

The Bible soundly refutes this notion. People of faith are people of hope because we have a personal Creator who has revealed himself to us and seeks a relationship with us. Our lives have meaning because God created us in his image with purpose. It makes sense that those who know God enjoy hope.

Scripture Reading...

HEBREWS 11:3

Study and Reflection

1. How do we know God created the universe? The Bible says
    so. "In the beginning God created the heavens and the
    earth. . . . And God said, 'Let there be light,' and there was
    light" (Gen. 1:1, 3). We join the ranks of those commended
    for their faith when we believe that God is our Creator. What
    do you learn from Abraham and the Apostle Paul's beliefs
    about our origin?

    a. "But Abram said to the king of Sodom, 'With raised
        hand I have sworn an oath to the LORD, God Most High,
        Creator of heaven and earth'" (Gen. 14:22).

    b. Paul said, "The God who made the world and everything
        in it is the Lord of heaven and earth and does not live
        in temples built by human hands. . . . Rather, he himself
        gives everyone life and breath and everything else. From
        one man he made all the nations, that they should inhabit
        the whole earth; and he marked out their appointed times
        in history and the boundaries of their lands. God did this
        so that they would seek him and perhaps reach out for
        him and find him, though he is not far from any one of
        us" (Acts 17:24–27).

2. According to the apostle Peter, what do God's scoffers
    forget? "They deliberately forget that God made the
    heavens long ago by the word of his command, and he

brought the earth out from the water and surrounded it with water" (2 Pet. 3:5 NLT).

3. What we believe about God affects our view of everything else. Looking at Hebrews 11:3, why does our view of the origin of life and the universe matter?

4. Has some aspect of creation left you in awe? Well then, are you ready for an even bigger *wow*? While God *spoke* worlds into being, he *knitted* you together in your mother's womb. Knitting is intricate and up close. "You made all the delicate, inner parts of my body and knit me together in my mother's womb. Thank you for making me so wonderfully complex! Your workmanship is marvelous—how well I know it. You watched me as I was being formed in utter seclusion, as I was woven together in the dark of the womb" (Ps. 139:13–15 NLT).

   a. What does this say about God's involvement in creating you?

   b. To believe God supervised our formation and knitted us together may take faith, especially in areas we wish we could change. Believing God designed us brings hope. I'm not a mistake—even my frailties. God shaped me with a special purpose for his glory. Like the psalmist, we can thank God for how he made us. Is there an area you need to begin looking at through faith? How would believing you are a marvelous work of God change the way you see yourself?

If God Is God . . .

Has anyone ever falsely accused you of lying? It hurts to have someone doubt your integrity—especially someone you care about. Let's turn that around. Have you ever doubted God?

When Satan tempted Eve, he questioned what God had said. Satan hasn't changed. He uses toeholds of doubt to manipulate us for his own purposes.

The Bible's first words say God spoke the world into being. It says each species will reproduce after its own kind (Gen. 1:24). This leaves room for microevolution within species but eliminates any possibility of macroevolution. Worms can't evolve into birds. And monkeys never became men. Far from being a grunting ape-man, the first man was brilliant. He invented names for all the animals and managed the Garden of Eden.

God's account is at odds with a culture that doesn't want to be accountable to a personal being. Who is the more reliable witness—God or humans?

I'm not a scientist, but I know the theory of evolution violates one of the core principles of science. All science is based on confirming or challenging theories through the observation of reproducible results through controlled experiments. Yet how can science explain the creation of the world and of humans when we cannot observe, replay, or reproduce our beginning?

We cannot prove the past through science. We know that events like Abraham Lincoln's Gettysburg Address and the assassination of John F. Kennedy are true because of eyewitness accounts. Creation had eyewitnesses too. Job 38:7 says the angels shouted for joy as they watched God create the world.

Honest scientific observations confirm Scripture instead of refuting it. Evolutionary changes can be seen *within* species but not from one species to another, affirming what the Bible said.

"And God said, 'Let the land produce living creatures according to their kinds'" (Gen. 1:24).

Anyone who's ever witnessed unattended lawns (or children) knows the need for intelligent intervention. Yards need gardeners, and children need supervision to thrive.

Years ago, at a holiday gathering, a friend pointed to a frozen container of cranberries and triumphantly declared, "Debbie, this is why I believe in evolution. Things just keep getting better!" Her statement stunned me, because in reality the container supported creation, not evolution. Cans of cranberry sauce don't slowly morph into frozen cranberry sauce. Someone with an idea on how to produce a fresher sauce *created* a new product.

There are many reasons a world system run by Satan wants us to doubt God. If we don't believe the first words he spoke in Genesis, which words will we believe? Old and New Testament believers recognized God as the Creator. Those who doubt God's ability to speak the world into being will also struggle to trust God in other areas.

Faith is only as reliable as its object. Jesus is "the Truth" (John 14:6). He is "the Word of God" (Rev. 19:13). He is the Creator: "Through him all things were made; without him nothing was made that has been made" (John 1:3). No one compares with him!

If God is God, then he is all the Bible proclaims:

- He is powerful enough to speak worlds into existence.
- His foolishness is wiser than our wisdom.
- His ways are higher—better—than ours.
- He makes no mistakes.
- He never lies.
- He is more loving than we can imagine, because God is love.
- He is righteous in his judgments.

- His word is true.
- He keeps his promises.

The men and women of faith discussed here trusted him. The question that remains for you and me is this: Will we trust him?

CLOSING PRAYER

Use this space to turn your insights and responses into prayers. You might begin with praying: *Lord, expand my vision of you. I choose to trust you. You are big enough to handle . . . (name your concerns).*

✳ my shoulder + my travel.

I Want to Remember . . .

Today's takeaways from #LittleFaithBigGod are:

Prayer Requests

F

The Most Important Thing to Know about Your Relationship with God

Abel means "breath" or "vapor."

Lambs nuzzled against Abel as he caressed their soft ears and examined each one. When he found a spot or flaw, he moved to the next lamb. After inspecting his flock, he nodded at one. "Perfect," he whispered. "You're the one."

A mocking laugh startled Abel. He tensed as he recognized his brother's sneer. "Brother, offer the lame one," Cain said. "Save the perfect one for breeding. Do you think God cares?"

"I care," Abel said as he led the lamb away. Oh, how he wished Cain cared.

IF I WERE COMPILING A LIST OF TESTIMONIES TO PROMOTE A product—say "Sparkling Body Wash"—I doubt I'd include the story of someone who died while using it. But God begins and ends the faith chapter, Hebrews 11, with martyrs. Adam and Eve's son Abel is the first person named in God's list of heroes, and he is history's first martyr.

Most of us are familiar with Cain and Abel. Previously, I'd only thought of their differences. But notice their similarities. Both brothers

- believed in God.
- worshipped (brought sacrifices) at the same time in the same place.
- knew what God wanted in worship.

The difference was in their faith. While Cain believed God existed, Abel also believed what God said. Only Abel

- recognized his need for a sacrifice.
- wanted to please God.
- followed God's instructions and, therefore, brought a better sacrifice.
- was commended as righteous.

The biblical account of Abel's life is brief. Yet God holds him up as an example of genuine faith in action. This week we'll see what we can learn about faith from Abel.

Day One
We Need a Sacrifice

Some of us are painfully aware of how often we fall short of our own standards, not to mention God's glory (Rom. 3:23). But whether we recognize our need or not, we each need a savior to deliver us from the power and consequences of sin.

God covered Adam and Eve with animal skins after they rebelled against him. Dr. Kent Hughes calls this "an implicit inference that animal blood was spilled in direct response to their sin."[1]

Noah and Abraham also offered animal sacrifices long before the Mosaic Law required them.

Throughout the Old Testament, God accepted many types of offerings, including grain offerings. But only blood offerings covered sin.

It's possible that animals communicated with Adam and Eve before the fall. Eve showed no surprise when the serpent spoke to her. It wasn't until after the great flood in Noah's day that the "fear and dread" of humans fell upon the animal kingdom (Gen. 9:2). We don't know if Adam and Eve saw God kill the animals, but at some point, they realized their sin had brought physical and spiritual death into the world. Could they have imagined that their sin would bring death to their son—and God's Son?

God had warned Adam, "you must not eat from the tree of the knowledge of good and evil, for when you eat from it you will certainly die" (Gen. 2:17). Romans 6:23 says, "the wages of sin is death." While Adam and Eve's physical death came hundreds of years later, their spiritual death was immediate. Since this act of disobedience, every human (except Jesus) has been born spiritually dead—alienated from God.

Adam and Eve must have explained the need for a sin offering to their sons. Cain and Abel both knew the place, the time, and the need for sacrifices. Cain brought "some of the fruits of the soil as an offering to the LORD. But Abel brought fat portions from some of the firstborn of his flock" (Gen. 4:3–4). Fat portions, firstborn, and first fruits represent the best portions. Cain brought God some, while Abel brought God his best.

How Cain and Abel worshipped showed what they believed about God. Abel respected God's holiness, mercy, and prescribed way to a relationship with him. "By faith Abel offered to God a better sacrifice than Cain, through which he obtained the testimony that he was righteous" (Heb. 11:4).

Cain sang "I Did It My Way" thousands of years before Frank Sinatra popularized the song. He was willing to bring offerings, but he wanted to do it his way. He reasoned that his collection of produce was as good as any bloody animal sacrifice. Jesus said, "Why do you call me, 'Lord, Lord,' and do not do what I say?" (Luke 6:46).

Abel's faith pleased God and provoked Cain (Gen. 4). Let's see how his faith relates to us and our relationship with God.

Scripture Reading...

HEBREWS 11:1, 2, 4
GENESIS 4:1–16

Study and Reflection

1. Both Cain and Abel brought offerings, but only Abel garnered God's favor (Gen. 4:1–5). According to Hebrews 11:1, 2, and 4, what specific trait made Abel and his sacrifice pleasing to God?

   Faith

2. What was missing from these people's worship? "These people honor me with their lips, but their hearts are far from me. They worship me in vain" (Matt. 15:8–9).

   Faith + heart / love of God only God.

3. Besides not bringing a blood offering, Cain didn't bring the best of his produce (Gen. 4:3–4). Consider the difference in how you approach buying a gift for someone you deeply love versus someone you hardly know. What do Cain's and Abel's respective offerings say about their relationships with God?

   did know good + did what he want told him to do. love God up all your heart mind + soul

4. Why is God's standard—faith—more reasonable and more challenging than being judged on the basis of our performance?

Because it is basic + doable

Why Blood Sacrifices?

A photograph of our son, Brant, covered in mud documents the special affinity my toddler had for puddles. The caked dirt didn't change my love for Brant. But it did affect how I treated him. He wasn't allowed to roam the house while muddy. I held him at arm's length when I carried him to a tub of running water. After he was clean, we snuggled close, and he gained free access inside the house again.

Who benefited from my child's bath? Bathing him was work for me, but it was also joy. Removing his grime restored the pleasure of cuddling together.

Some people avoid God when they mess up. They think he doesn't want to see them. But Jesus died to remove the stench of sin that separated us. He wants to share life now and throughout eternity.

Before sin entered the world, there was no need for sacrifices. After sin, animal sacrifices provided a temporary remedy so people could enjoy closeness with God. From the skin garments God made to clothe the first man and woman to the blood sacrifices that were part of the Mosaic Law, blood was God's provision for removing guilt and restoring fellowship with him (Lev. 17:11). "In fact, . . . without the shedding of blood there is no forgiveness" (Heb. 9:22).

Like bathing with body wash, the effectiveness of animal sacrifices was temporary. These Old Testament sacrifices pointed to the sacrifice of God's perfect Lamb who would conquer sin on our behalf:

- "With his own blood—not the blood of goats and calves—he entered the Most Holy Place once for all time and secured our redemption forever" (Heb. 9:12 NLT).
- "Just think how much more the blood of Christ will purify our consciences from sinful deeds so that we can worship the living God. For by the power of the eternal Spirit, Christ offered himself to God as a perfect sacrifice for our sins" (Heb. 9:14 NLT).
- "But now, once for all time, he has appeared at the end of the age to remove sin by his own death as a sacrifice" (Heb. 9:26 NLT).

John MacArthur said Abel's sacrifice prefigured the way of the cross.

- Abel offered "—one lamb for one person.
- Later came the Passover—with one lamb for one family.
- Then came the Day of Atonement—with one lamb for one nation.
- Finally came Good Friday—one Lamb for the whole world."[2]

When John the Baptist pointed to Jesus and said, "Look, the Lamb of God, who takes away the sin of the world!" (John 1:29), his Jewish audience understood. This was the long-awaited One first promised to Adam and Eve (Gen. 3:15).

While we look back in history to the cross, Old Testament believers offered sacrifices that pointed to his coming. Both Old and New Testament believers held faith in God's promised One, leading them along the path of righteousness. When we accept Jesus's sacrifice for our sin, like Abel, we please God and gain his eternal approval.

CLOSING PRAYER

Use this space to turn your insights and responses into prayers.

acceptance of Jesus doesn't take performance; It is in the our heart.

I Want to Remember . . .

What do you want to remember from today's study? Let's encourage each other by sharing our takeaways on social media with the hashtag #LittleFaithBigGod.

Day Two

We Miss the Mark

The spiders on our wooded lot hadn't gotten the memo that we weren't decorating for Halloween. Lacy webs embellished our front porch in spite of my effort to sweep them away. A thirty-inch web greeted me when I walked my guests outside to say goodnight. How could I have missed this embarrassing display? Had it appeared during their visit? More likely, my porch lights exposed the gossamer previously hidden by shadows.

The Bible says, "Everyone who does evil hates the light, and will not come into the light for fear that their deeds will be exposed" (John 3:20). Cain tried to hide his dark heart behind perfunctory worship. When exposed, he repelled closeness with God. He shunned God's warning and invitation to do right. Cain preferred to sulk over God's rejection of his half-hearted worship than to change. Even after murdering his brother, he showed no remorse. Instead, he hid behind the "I'm a victim of unjust punishment" complaint.

It's obvious Cain needed cleansing, but why did Abel need a sacrifice? Compared with Cain, Abel looked good.

The Bible doesn't explain Abel's sin, but he knew he needed cleansing. Perhaps fellowship with God exposed the dust that sin had deposited in his soul, just as my porch light revealed delicate webs. Abel accepted God's assessment and provision for cleansing. And God declared him righteous (Heb. 11:4).

Have you heard people say that they believe they'll go to heaven because they've lived a good life? Maybe you've felt that way. How good must a person be to go to heaven? Let's look at what Abel knew about sin that will help us in our worship.

Scripture Reading...
HEBREWS 11:4

Study and Reflection

1. If we fail to recognize sin's influence in our lives, we won't understand our need for the Savior. From the following, why is it impossible to enter heaven and live close to God based on our performance?

    a. "All of us have become like one who is unclean, and all our righteous acts are like filthy rags" (Isa. 64:6).

    b. "You have heard that it was said, 'You shall not commit adultery.' But I tell you that anyone who looks at a woman lustfully has already committed adultery with her in his heart" (Matt. 5:27–28).

c. "But I tell you that anyone who is angry with a brother or sister will be subject to judgment. . . . And anyone who says, 'You fool!' will be in danger of the fire of hell" (Matt. 5:22).

d. "Be perfect, therefore, as your heavenly Father is perfect" (Matt. 5:48).

e. "Everything that does not come from faith is sin" (Rom. 14:23).

f. "For whoever keeps the whole law and yet stumbles at just one point is guilty of breaking all of it" (James 2:10).

2. If God allowed imperfection into his home, it would no longer be heaven. The previous verses explained why it's impossible to enter heaven based on human righteousness. What's God's solution for our sin problem?

a. "But he [Jesus] was pierced for our rebellion, crushed for our sins. He was beaten so we could be whole. He was whipped so we could be healed. All of us, like sheep, have strayed away. We have left God's paths to follow our own. Yet the Lord laid on him the sins of us all. . . . When he sees all that is accomplished by his anguish, he will be satisfied. And because of his experience, my righteous servant will make it possible for many to be counted righteous, for he will bear all their sins" (Isa. 53:5–6, 11 NLT).

b. "For God made Christ, who never sinned, to be the offering for our sin, so that we could be made right with God through Christ" (2 Cor. 5:21 NLT).

3. What must we do? "Believe in the Lord Jesus, and you will be saved—you and your household" (Acts 16:31).

How God Sees Sin

In January 2017, the news reported a shooting in the Fort Lauderdale airport that killed at least five people and wounded others. Grief for the victims and their families and anger toward the killer punched my stomach. One of our friends was scheduled to fly into Florida that next day.

Hearing they had the suspect in custody offered some relief. *He deserves whatever he gets*, I thought.

A couple of hours later, my daughter told me the suspect was reported to be a soldier who'd returned from Iraq as a troubled man. My emotions flipped as I recalled the helplessness of a young client from my biblical counseling practice. Her husband had also returned from war a shell of the man he'd been. Images of him holding his dying buddy in his arms crossed my mind.

Life is so messy. Only Jesus can accurately judge sin.

We tend to weigh our best intentions against another's worst actions to justify ourselves. But God doesn't measure our sin by comparing us with each other.

God looks into our hearts. He sees our motives. That's why even angry words and unkind thoughts matter. While muttering "idiot" under our breath to the cyclist who darted in front of our car is better than running over him in a fit of road rage, both reveal the presence of sin. A nature so easily irritated is capable of indescribable evil under the right provocation.

My snap judgment on the airport killer seemed proper, based on the bleeding bodies and bereaved families. But only Jesus knows the demons the shooter was fighting in his head during his rampage. Only Jesus can judge a soul.

No Small Sin

A cavalier attitude toward sin indicates a superficial understanding of the extensive ramifications of sin—and grace. Every sin is a capital offense that must be paid for either by our own eternal death or by Jesus's substitutionary death on the cross (Rom. 6:23). No one can stand before a holy God on the basis of his or her righteousness. "There is no one righteous, not even one" (Rom. 3:10).

How God Views Righteousness

God judged our sins—past, present, and future—on the cross. When we accept Jesus's perfect sacrifice on our behalf, God gives us his Son's perfect score. God does not weigh our good deeds against our bad ones. He weighs our sin by whether we've trusted or rejected Jesus. We either trust the blood of Christ to cleanse us or, like Cain, eventually learn our efforts didn't earn God's approval.

Abel's sacrifice demonstrated faith in God's provision. The more I come to understand sin's pervasive influence, the more I appreciate Jesus. Like the woman who washed his feet with her tears, realizing how much I've been forgiven causes me to love him more (Luke 7:40–48).

CLOSING PRAYER

Use this space to turn your insights and responses into prayers. If you are uncertain that you belong to Christ, why not agree with God that you've fallen short of his glory? Thank him for sending

Jesus to the cross to pay for your sins. Invite Jesus to be your Lord and Savior.

I Want to Remember . . .

Today's takeaways from #LittleFaithBigGod are:

Day Three
God Is Precise

In an old commercial, a room full of people hush when a man says, "My broker is E. F. Hutton. And E. F. Hutton says . . ."

"When E. F. Hutton talks people listen," says the commentator.

Dining with a large group, I felt like I was in an E. F. Hutton ad when the man next to me said, "You know, the longer I live, the more I can't imagine a loving God turning anyone away from heaven just because they don't believe in Jesus. Can you?"

Time froze as the image of Jesus on the night of his betrayal popped into my mind. I pictured him sweating drops of blood as "He offered up both prayers and supplications with loud crying and tears to the One able to save Him from death" (Heb. 5:7 NASB).

I looked at my companion and reminded him that Jesus had asked if it were possible to avoid the cross (Matt. 26:36–56). "I can't imagine a loving Father forcing his only Son to die on a cross if there was any other way to God."

"I never thought of it that way," he said and turned away to talk with someone else.

When God seems narrow, it's safe to say we're looking at the situation from the wrong perspective. Maybe it's better to say he is precise. He knows what works and what doesn't.

Scripture Reading..
JOHN 4:24

Study and Reflection

1. What constitutes true worship to God? Cain and Abel both brought sacrifices. *spirit filled.*

   a. "Does the LORD delight in burnt offerings and sacrifices as much as in obeying the LORD? To obey is better than sacrifice, and to heed is better than the fat of rams. For rebellion is like the sin of divination, and arrogance like the evil of idolatry" (1 Sam. 15:22–23).

      obey the Lord via spirit

   b. David wrote after his sin against Bathsheba, "My sacrifice, O God, is a broken spirit; a broken and contrite heart you, God, will not despise" (Ps. 51:17).

2. How has Jesus's sacrifice changed the way we approach God?

   a. "No one else can save us. Indeed, we can be saved only by the power of the one named Jesus and not by any other person" (Acts 4:12 GWT).

b. "Let us then approach God's throne of grace with confidence, so that we may receive mercy and find grace to
help us in our time of need" (Heb. 4:16).

3. Why do we no longer offer sacrifices for sin? "First he said,
'Sacrifices and offerings, burnt offerings and sin offerings you
did not desire, nor were you pleased with them'—though
they were offered in accordance with the law. Then he [Jesus]
said, 'Here I am, I have come to do your will.' He sets aside
the first to establish the second. And by that will, we have
been made holy through the sacrifice of the body of Jesus
Christ once for all" (Heb. 10:8–10). Final sacrifice

4. God declared Abel righteous on the basis of his faith (Heb.
11:4), faith that was manifested in his offering to God. On
what basis are we declared righteous?

a. "Therefore, if anyone is in Christ, the new creation has
come: The old has gone, the new is here! . . . God made
him who had no sin to be sin for us, so that in him we
might become the righteousness of God" (2 Cor. 5:17, 21).

b. "For it is by grace you have been saved, through faith—
and this is not from yourselves, it is the gift of God—not
by works, so that no one can boast" (Eph. 2:8–9).

5. If you were in a burning building with no way of escape
and a firefighter fought his way in to save you, would you

complain about the route out? Those who don't appreciate God's provision don't realize what Jesus has saved us from and what it cost him. According to the following excerpts, what has Christ saved us from and what did it cost him?

a. "For you know that God paid a ransom to save you from the empty life you inherited from your ancestors. And it was not paid with mere gold or silver, which lose their value. It was the precious blood of Christ, the sinless, spotless Lamb of God" (1 Pet. 1:18–19 NLT).

b. "The Son of Man will send out his angels, and they will weed out of his kingdom everything that causes sin and all who do evil. They will throw them into the blazing furnace, where there will be weeping and gnashing of teeth" (Matt. 13:41–42).

6. "Now faith is confidence in what we hope for and assurance about what we do not see" (Heb. 11:1). How can we know for sure that we will go to heaven when we die?

a. "For God so loved the world that he gave his one and only Son, that whoever believes in him shall not perish but have eternal life. For God did not send his Son into the world to condemn the world, but to save the world through him. Whoever believes in him is not condemned, but whoever does not believe stands condemned already because they have not believed in the name of God's one and only Son" (John 3:16–19).

b. "Whoever has the Son has life; whoever does not have the Son of God does not have life. These things I have written to you who believe in the name of the Son of God, so that you may know that you have eternal life" (1 John 5:12–13).

7. God doesn't owe us a way of escape from the judgment we earned. But he's provided one and made the path clear so we won't be deceived by other voices. Knowing salvation is in no one else spares us from wasted effort and uncertainty. Yet, like Cain, people still challenge the idea of a narrow path to life. What thoughts do you have on this?

The Pain of Becoming Sin

When I visited Yad Vashem—The World Holocaust Remembrance Center in Jerusalem—story after story of needless cruelty crushed me. A picture of a smiling mother and her two-year-old son was followed with the story of how the Nazis separated them from each other and sent them to different camps before murdering them both. I left a weeping mess. If just reading short snippets of those World War II horrors pained me, I can only imagine what it was like to live them. Jesus did more than live them; blameless Jesus, who never had an impure thought, became each horrendous sin.

The agony Jesus experienced on the cross sliced much deeper than the physical pain of crucifixion. Jesus took on every sin that has been or ever will be committed. That means he took the sins that have been committed against us, as well as the ones we've committed. He suffered in a few hours what would take the rest of us an eternity to suffer. He took the hell we deserve so we could share his heaven.

Romanian pastor Richard Wurmbrand endured daily beatings while in a Communist prison. The atrocities he experienced and witnessed cannot compare with the wrath Jesus took for us, but they do provide a glimpse into Christ's incomparable love: "I have seen Christians in Communist prisons with fifty pounds of chains on their feet, tortured with red-hot iron pokers, in whose throats spoonfuls of salt had been forced, being kept afterward without water, starving, whipped, suffering from cold—and praying with fervor for the Communists."[3]

When Wurmbrand preached about the cross to those behind the Iron Curtain, he said there was not a dry eye. When he came to the West and preached the cross, there was not a wet eye. Perhaps only those who know anguish can fully appreciate the One who willingly suffered for them.

Study the founder of any religion and you will discover a flawed person who needed a savior. Jesus is the only person since Adam and Eve who was born spiritually alive and without sin. He is the only one who can supply spiritual life.

If there had been another way to save us, Jesus would have skipped the cross. But there was no other way. Today, we still choose between the way of the cross and the way of Cain.

CLOSING PRAYER

Use this space to turn your insights and responses into prayers.

I Want to Remember . . .

Today's takeaways from #LittleFaithBigGod are:

Christ is the sacrifice, not need & sacrifice or works to save us. faith alone

Day Four

My Way Won't Work

Cain means "possession."

Cain believed he could earn God's favor through what he did. I believed I could lose his favor by what I didn't do—until God showed me better.

As a single gal in ministry, I enjoyed my work and spent my waking hours with students. After marriage, I wanted to spend my evenings with my husband. Larry supervised teams in other states, and sometimes I traveled with him. I enjoyed this—until I had to fill out ministry forms. Writing zeros in my weekly report turned my stomach.

There were no boxes to check for being a supportive wife. In my desire to be a fruitful Christian, I had unwittingly equated service for God with approval by God. The low numbers in my columns showed my disappointing approval rating. Guilt distanced me from God. Who wants to spend time with someone you think is disappointed in you?

The Lord brought me to my senses as I read Galatians 3:1–3: "You foolish Galatians! Who has bewitched you? Before your very eyes Jesus Christ was clearly portrayed as crucified. I would like to learn just one thing from you: Did you receive the Spirit by the works of the law, or by believing what you heard? Are you so foolish? After beginning by means of the Spirit, are you now trying to finish by means of the flesh?"

I'd done nothing to earn God's love; I could do nothing to make him love me more—or less. Jesus's performance, not mine, was the basis of my acceptance and righteousness before God (Titus 3:4–6). His Word, not a ministry report, settled the matter.

My weekly report formed my standard of approval. How do you measure your value? Is it by your job title, dress size, or how well your kids are doing? Often, we don't recognize we have these standards until we fail to meet them.

I could have told you that unbelievers can't stand before a holy God based on their deeds. I just didn't realize that as a believer, I was trying to do exactly that. Perhaps you need a reminder too. We weren't saved by grace through faith to be approved by works. Faith and grace are the Christian's way of life: "This Good News tells us how God makes us right in his sight. This is accomplished from start to finish by faith. As Scripture says, 'It is through faith that a righteous person has life'" (Rom. 1:17 NLT). Did you catch that? From "start to finish by faith." My failure to meet my own standards uncovered the lies I believed about the source of my righteousness and softened my heart to receive the truth.

We Can't Earn Acceptance

Let's settle this once and for all. We will never be good enough to earn God's acceptance. Saints aren't people who never sin. Dr. Neil Anderson, founder and president emeritus of Freedom in Christ Ministries and formerly chairman of the Practical Theology Department at Talbot School of Theology, explains, "As believers, we are not trying to become saints; we are saints who are becoming like Christ." Dr. Anderson adds, "Our relationship with God is based on the blood of the Lord Jesus Christ. We are saved by how we believe, not by how we behave."[4]

The Bible calls believers saints and unbelievers sinners. Still, many Christians identify themselves as "sinners" because they know they aren't perfect. But, as my experience demonstrated, such a view affects how we relate to God. Calling myself a sinner diminishes Jesus's finished work on the cross. Do I believe my misdeeds are stronger than Christ's work in me and on my behalf?

Romans 5:15–17 contradicts this by describing the "much more" effect of God's grace. John 3:1–2 says we are *children of God* even though we have *not yet* become all that we will be.

Child or Criminal

Think about your life. Do you see God as a loving Father when you feel good about yourself and a stern judge when you're unhappy with yourself? In other words, does your relationship with God hinge on your behavior?

Paul writes, "So now there is no condemnation for those who belong to Christ Jesus" (Rom. 8:1 NLT). You may be thinking, *Easy for Paul to say. He was an apostle.* Think again. This verse follows Paul's confession of how he failed to do the good he wanted to do and did the very wrong he didn't want to do.

We become children of God by grace through faith (John 1:12; Eph. 2:8). He doesn't throw us out of his family when we mess up (Rom. 8:15). He knew everything about us *before* he chose us in Christ Jesus.

Believing Unbelievers

The Lord reached out to Cain and showed him how to be accepted. He warned that sin would devour him if he didn't take action. But Cain preferred to nurse his outrage instead of heed God's help.

As Scottish author George MacDonald wrote in *The Princess and Curdie,* "A beast does not know that he is a beast, and the nearer a man gets to being a beast, the less he knows it." Cain's petrified heart showed no contrition. He was condemned not for being in darkness but for refusing to leave the darkness: "But anyone who keeps on sinning does not know him or understand who he is" (1 John 3:6). It's no surprise that Cain eventually walked away from God all together.

Scripture Reading...
GENESIS 4:5–16

Study and Reflection

1. What impresses you about God's interaction with Cain in Genesis 4:5–7? Notice who initiated the conversation after God rejected Cain's offering.

2. What would have lifted Cain's countenance and saved him from greater pain (verses 5–7)?

3. How do God's instructions to Cain apply to us (verse 7)?

4. God gave Cain the freedom to reject his warning, and he extends the same to us. Even after Cain murdered Abel, God reached out to him again. How did Cain respond to God's questions (verse 9)?

5. What happens when we try to hide our sin? "Whoever conceals their sins does not prosper, but the one who confesses and renounces them finds mercy" (Prov. 29:13).

6. God took Abel to paradise and applauded his faith. What happened to Cain (verses 10–12)?

7. The ground that soaked up Abel's blood quit producing food for Cain. The penalties of our sins are often built into the sin. You break a confidence and lose a friendship. While we may not be able to predict where a wrong choice will lead, we can usually trace it backward. Can you think of examples where ignoring God's wisdom led to painful consequences?

8. How did God show mercy to unrepentant Cain in his judgment (verses 13–15)?

9. Cain and King David, who were both responsible for the murder of innocent men, gave opposite responses when confronted for their sins (Gen. 4:5, 13, 14, and Psalm 32:1–5). How might Cain's outcome have been different if he'd confessed and renounced his sin?

10. Consider all those who suffered because of Cain's sin. Who suffers when we sin?

The Way of Cain Is the Way of Pain

A neighborhood child, whom I'll call Abby, was in my daughter's first-grade class. Abby's father left her mother—and her—for another woman. Abby, in turn, lashed out against the neighborhood children.

Who did this man's adultery hurt? His wife and child obviously grieved. But my children also suffered. The sin committed by a man we'd never met disrupted our neighborhood and his daughter's classroom. Believing we can corral the consequences of our private sins is like throwing a flaming, gasoline-soaked rag into an apartment and being astonished when the whole building burns down. Did we think it would only singe the carpet?

The freedom to choose carries responsibility. Our decisions affect others, sometimes for generations. And sin always grieves God and harms the one sinning.

It is difficult to understand why God let Cain reject his warning when it meant death for Abel, Adam and Eve's righteous son. But God also let Adam and Eve violate his command when it meant death for his Son.

God rejected Cain's half-hearted offering but showed him how he could be accepted. Cain spurned God and murdered Abel. This increased Cain's misery. The blood he spilled cursed the ground he tilled. Every failed crop reminded him of his sin.

We don't know how much Abel suffered at Cain's hand, but his life was cut short. Adam and Eve lost two sons that day. The consequences of Cain's sin drove him and his wife to become restless wanderers and infected his descendants (Gen. 4:23–24).

Cain demonstrated the truth of this Proverb: "But he who sins against me injures himself; All those who hate me love death" (Prov. 8:36 NASB).

Even though some consequences of sin play out on earth, the death of God's Son brings forgiveness to all who receive him. No one has to stay in sin.

CLOSING PRAYER

Use this space to turn your insights and responses into prayers.

I Want to Remember . . .

Today's takeaways from #LittleFaithBigGod are:

Day Five

Getting the Last Word

"What we do in life echoes in eternity."
—Maximus from the movie *Gladiator*

Cain had no argument that could stand before God, so to get the last word, he silenced his brother. Did he think he'd look better without Abel around? The Bible says Cain murdered his brother because "his deeds were evil, and his brother's were righteous" (1 John 3:12).

Evil must extinguish the light that exposes it. My husband once mentored a new believer who admitted that before knowing Christ, he'd padded his expense account at work. After Jesus transformed his life, he wanted to repay the amount he'd wrongly reimbursed.

He confessed to his boss, who promptly fired him. The rest of the company still cushioned their accounts. To continue their dishonesty, they had to remove this man.

Sometimes we suffer for doing the right thing. It smarts. But knowing that a perpetrator will get away with a wrongdoing burns on a whole other level. We replay scenarios in our minds, hoping to nail our accuser and exonerate ourselves with the perfect last word.

The Bible says, "The memory of the righteous is blessed, but the name of the wicked will rot" (Prov. 10:7 NASB). It also says the righteous "will be remembered forever" (Ps. 112:6). Thousands of years after Abel's death, Jesus and other New Testament passages remembered him. In fact, Abel's life still speaks today. Righteousness gets the last word.

Scripture Reading...

GENESIS 4:5–16

Study and Reflection

1. Cain was Abel's brother. They "worshipped" at the same place. Yet Cain was dangerous. What applications do you draw from the following verses?

    a. "By this the children of God and the children of the devil are obvious: anyone who does not practice righteousness is not of God, nor the one who does not love his brother. For this is the message which you have heard from the beginning, that we should love one another; not as Cain, who was of the evil one and slew his brother. And for what reason did he slay him? Because his deeds were evil, and his brother's were righteous" (1 John 3:10–12 NASB).

    b. "Woe to them! They have taken the way of Cain. . . . 'See, the Lord is coming with thousands upon thousands of his holy ones to judge everyone, and to convict all of them of all the ungodly acts they have committed in their ungodliness, and of all the defiant words ungodly sinners have spoken against him'" (Jude 1:11, 14–15).

2. Jesus remembered Abel. What do you take from his words
   spoken to the hypocritical religious leaders of his day?
   "Therefore this generation will be held responsible for the
   blood of all the prophets that has been shed since the beginning of the world, from the blood of Abel to the blood of
   Zechariah, who was killed between the altar and the sanctu-
   ary. Yes, I tell you, this generation will be held responsible for
   it all" (Luke 11:50–51; see also Matt. 23:35).

The Blood of Abel and the Blood of Jesus Speak

"To Jesus the mediator of a new covenant, and to the sprinkled
blood that speaks a better word than the blood of Abel" (Heb. 12:24).

We've contrasted Cain and Abel's worship. Notice the difference
between Christ's and Abel's blood.

Abel's blood condemns those who, like Cain, destroy good
people because they themselves are evil. But Jesus's blood saves
whoever comes to him in faith. Jesus's blood speaks cleansing,
recovery, and hope. Jesus's blood secured justice and paid for the
sins of the world. It proclaims redemption to all who trust him.
Christ's blood changes us from enemies to beloved children of
God. And while Abel was murdered, Jesus laid down his life for
his sheep (John 10:17–18).

Abel Still Speaks

Both Cain and Abel believed God existed and brought him sacrifices. But Cain demanded to be accepted on the basis of his religious
activity, whereas Abel worshipped by faith.

Paul wrote about two other brothers, sons of Abraham: "At that
time the son born according to the flesh persecuted the son born
by the power of the Spirit. It is the same now" (Gal. 4: 29). People

who practice religion can feel entitled before God. They resent and attack those who serve Jesus out of joy and gratitude, unshackled by a heavy sense of duty.

Cain killed his brother, but he couldn't silence him. Abel, "though he is dead, he still speaks" (Heb. 11:4). What does Abel say?

- We worship because God is worthy, not to prove our worth.
- Faith, not religious activity, gives us right-standing with God.
- A life that pleases God offends the wicked—especially the religious wicked.
- Sometimes good people suffer because they are good.
- God deals justly with those who prey on his children.
- Suffering for Christ will pass, but a godly testimony will last.
- God remembers the faithful.

Unlike the limits of animal blood, Jesus's blood never stops working. Like a spiritual cleanser, it continues to disinfect us from sin so that we can enjoy unbroken fellowship with God. The way of the cross spotlights Jesus instead of our sin. God wants us to be Christ-focused, not sin-focused. The way of the cross seems narrow to those who haven't taken that path. But those washed by the blood find it liberating.

When we come to God his way, we know that he, not our sin, gets the last word.

Next week, Enoch will show us how to enjoy God's company.

CLOSING PRAYER

Use this space to turn your insights and responses into prayers.

I Want to Remember . . .

Today's takeaways from #LittleFaithBigGod are:

Prayer Requests

Jesus Pursues the Pleasure of Your Company

Enoch means "dedicated."

A flock of honking geese glided overhead and splashed into the water. Enoch smiled, then sighed. The pink streaks from the sinking sun were beautiful, but they signaled it was time to head home. He pulled his robe around his neck as he prepared to leave.

"When I'm with you, Lord, time vanishes. Does that have anything to do with you being eternal?" He smiled again, then bowed his head, "Lord, I think I understand the ache this beauty awakens. I'm homesick—homesick for you."

PICTURES OF NOAH AND THE ARK GRACE CHILDREN'S NURS-eries and church classrooms, but Enoch is less familiar. Enoch's claim to fame is that he did not experience death.

I find it refreshing that God holds up Enoch as an example of faith. Skipping death is pretty remarkable by any standard. But Enoch couldn't have arranged that. What was his part in this amazing account? "Enoch walked faithfully with God" (Gen. 5:24).

Enoch has become one of my favorite examples of faith. The record of his life shows that God enjoys the pleasure of our company.

Day One

God Seeks the Pleasure of Your Company

Accomplishments and activity don't impress God. Do I hear a collective sigh from all of us driven types? You don't have to be Type A to feel the pressure to do more. Just attend most churches, at least in the South. Merely listening to the announcements at a church where my husband and I were to speak sucked the energy out of me. You would have thought every child in the church was headed to hell because the faithful who'd shown up for the service weren't working in the nursery.

News flash: we aren't saved by grace to be sanctified by works. Genuine faith expresses itself through action, and we are "created in Christ Jesus to do good works" (Eph. 2:10), but God-pleasing works are faith powered. Works fueled by guilt or selfish ambition never please him. To walk with God, we must resist the pressures of the world—including the religious world—that applaud human *doings* instead of human *beings*.

God enjoyed the pleasure of Enoch's company. Can you think of anything sweeter than that? Let's personalize that: God seeks the pleasure of *your* company.

Scripture Reading...

GENESIS 5:21–24

HEBREWS 11:5–6

Study and Reflection

1. What do you observe about Enoch?

   Faithful later in life, recognized for walking w/ God. personal relationship.

w

★ witness ★

Commended
He was

2. For what was he commended (Heb. 11:5)?

Did not die = was taken up. = Pleasing
Faithfulness —   to God.

3. Enoch was the son of Jared, who descended from Adam and
Eve through the line of Seth (Gen. 5:7–18), not to be con-
fused with another Enoch who was Cain's son (Gen. 4:17).
In contrast to Seth's godly line, Cain's ungodly line boasted
many accomplishments. Cain founded a city, Jabal was the
first to raise livestock, Jubal was the first to play the harp
and flute, and Tubal-Cain was an expert in forging tools of
bronze and iron (Gen. 4:17–22). In spite of these achievements, God commended none of these men. What does
this tell you about how God, in contrast to the world, mea-
sures success? *The world measure are not*
★ seen; rewarded by God.

4. What lessons and personal applications do you draw from
Enoch's life? *Content that I do not want to achieve.* */ please God.*

For What Will You Be Remembered?

We want to know our lives and work matter. So when I'm around
people who have the energy and talent to accomplish more than
I do, I'm tempted to compare myself with their accomplishments
and feel insignificant.

But the Bible doesn't tout bigger or more as necessarily better;
nor does it say smaller is less important. God's story includes public
figures and private intercessors. What matters to the Lord is being
faithful in every season of life. Living to please him, instead of to
impress people or build a name for ourselves, frees us to enjoy the

life he has for us and to say no to opportunities that don't line up with his will for us.

The impressive accomplishments of Cain's family line made them successes in the world's eyes. In contrast, the Bible remembers Enoch not for heroic achievements but for his fellowship with God. The difference is striking, and so is the message. Do I yearn to hear "well done" from the world or from God?

God wants the pleasure of our company. Would it be enough to be remembered as one who pleased God?

CLOSING PRAYER

Use this space to turn your insights and responses into prayers.

Please put my eyes to you oh God & look towards pleasing you

I Want to Remember . . .

What do you want to remember from today's study? Let's encourage each other by sharing our takeaways on social media with the hashtag #LittleFaithBigGod.

Day Two
God Wants to Be Found

My favorite "hide-and-seek" games took place at night with my older cousins at a friend's log cabin on the marsh. The salty air, twinkling lightning bugs, and the moon shining over the water created a magical setting for our childhood play. We scrambled to disappear, hoping the seeker would give up looking.

When Hebrews says God "rewards those who earnestly seek him," we may picture a game of "hide-and-seek." However, since God wants to be found, let's consider another analogy.

Do you remember what it was like to fall in love? You learned all you could about the object of your affection. You perked up when he or she walked into the room. You noticed his habits. You knew his favorite hangouts and just happened to show up when he'd be there. And if the feeling was mutual, he left hints that turned into invitations to join him. He beamed when you arrived and returned the attention.

Jesus is the lover of our souls who woos us. He is the Bridegroom who delights with the anticipation of a lover when we seek him. He rejoices when we thrill at his whisper and learn all we can about him. He longs to share stories, secrets, and life with us. He is not hiding from us.

In fact, the Bible shows God as the seeker. He looks for the lost and hiding.

Scripture Reading..
HEBREWS 11:5–6

Study and Reflection

1. Enoch was known as a person who pleased God. Connecting Enoch with Hebrews 11:6, what do we know to be true about him? By faith · witnesses that he was pleasing to God ; Find out all I can do to please God

2. What does it mean to seek God sincerely? by faith / made out whole heart · ✗

3. In the following verses, circle the seeker and underline the
    one who is hiding or lost.

    a. "But the Lord God called to the man [Adam after he'd
        sinned], 'Where are you?'" (Gen. 3:9).
    b. "Then the Lord said to Cain, 'Why are you angry? Why is
        your face downcast? If you do what is right, will you not
        be accepted?'" (Gen. 4:6–7).
    c. "Suppose one of you shepherds has a hundred sheep
        and loses one of them. Doesn't he leave the ninety-nine
        in the open country and go after the lost sheep until he
        finds it? And when he finds it, he joyfully puts it on his
        shoulders and goes home. Then he calls his friends and
        neighbors together and says, 'Rejoice with me; I have
        found my lost sheep.' I tell you that in the same way there
        will be more rejoicing in heaven over one sinner who
        repents than over ninety-nine righteous persons who do
        not need to repent" (Luke 15:3–7).
    d. "Here I [Jesus] am! I stand at the door and knock. If
        anyone hears my voice and opens the door, I will come in
        and eat with that person, and they with me" (Rev. 3:20).

4. Has today's reading expanded or changed what you think it
    means to seek God sincerely? If so, how?

    Listen

    Simplify my life + prayers.
    seek God by Faith

    Direct
    Deliber
    Sweet

God Sought Us First!

Did you know closeness with God is healing for your body as
well as your soul? In *Radical Remission,* Kelly Turner shares her
findings after interviewing cancer patients classified with sponta-
neous remission. These patients didn't believe their healing was

unprompted, because they worked for it. One surprising key factor these patients shared in common was knowing they weren't alone.[1]

We were created for relationship. Turner learned that, for some, these relationships included family and friends. For others, it was a dedicated spouse. And for still others, closeness with God was all they needed to know they weren't alone.

God designed us to share life with him. We seek God in response to him first seeking us. Notice how God pursues a relationship with us even when we fail:

- He called to Adam and Eve, "Where are you?" when they hid from him after their disobedience (Gen. 3:9).
- He sought angry Cain after he'd messed up, twice (Gen. 4:6–7, 9).
- He's the Good Shepherd searching for the lost sheep (Luke 15:3–7).
- He's the Father running to welcome his prodigal child home (Luke 15:11–21).
- He stands knocking at the door of our hearts waiting for us to invite him in (Rev. 3:20).

God is not hiding from us. He pursues us with love. He invites us to seek him so we can know him through experience—know his company, counsel, and comfort. Don't you want to know such a God?

CLOSING PRAYER

Use this space to turn your insights and responses into prayers.

I Want to Remember . . .

Today's takeaways from #LittleFaithBigGod are:

Day Three
God Shares Special Insights

Too often, I'm more eager to find an answer to a problem than to experience God in my difficulty. I want a solution—now. But gnawing on my problem, like a dog on a rawhide chew, never satisfies me.

Hebrews 11:6 says God rewards those who seek him. Jesus invites us to bring our burdens to him. He wants to carry them, but he also longs to connect with us. Imagine how close you'd feel to someone who only called when she needed something. A real friend wants a relationship, not just an answer.

When I give my problems and desires to Jesus and trust him to guide me, I experience supernatural peace. He is the Prince of Peace, and the fellowship of his company is sweeter than the answer to my prayer.

The Bible highlights Enoch for his close companionship with God. Enoch didn't start walking with God until he was sixty-five. After that, Enoch stuck with God through the ups and downs of life. God was more than a problem solver. He was Enoch's closest friend. The relationship "pleased God" (Heb. 11:5).

Do you want to know the secret of their friendship? Enoch lived every day believing that "God exists and that he rewards those who sincerely seek him" (Heb. 11:6 NLT). He sought God, along with his opinion and perspective in the various areas of life. He knew God would reward his seeking.

So how do we seek God in our busy lives? One way is to ask him to reveal himself to us and then to look for him. When we read the Bible, we must ask ourselves what we learned about him in the passage we read. That may sound obvious, but I don't always do that. When I pause to consider what I learned about him, I often see new things.

For example, after reading Genesis 39:21—"the Lord was with him [Joseph]; he showed him kindness and granted him favor in the eyes of the prison warden"—I realized that when people are kind to me, it is because God is kind to me. This helped me to recognize his activity in my daily life.

Seeking God caused Enoch's love for the Lord to overshadow his desire for anything else. I wonder if God asked Enoch if he wanted to go home with him the day he was "no more." Or did Enoch ask if he could stay with God? It was so natural to be in God's company; I wonder if he noticed the moment his feet left earth.

God may not reward us the same way he did Enoch, but God hasn't changed. He still rewards those who earnestly seek him. And those who trust him still make him smile.

Scripture Reading..

GENESIS 5:21–22
HEBREWS 11:5–6

Study and Reflection

1. What is the difference between seeking an answer and seeking God? Do your prayers include both (Phil. 4:6–7)?

   seeking god may not provide an answer we understand or expected yes my prayers usually include both

2. What event may have precipitated Enoch's walk with God (Gen. 5:21–22)? *Birth of Methusalah + other Sons + Daughters.*

3. What special revelation did God give this Old Testament believer that is yet to be fulfilled? "Enoch, the seventh from Adam, prophesied about them: 'See, the Lord is coming with thousands upon thousands of his holy ones to judge everyone, and to convict all of them of all the ungodly acts they have committed in their ungodliness, and of all the defiant words ungodly sinners have spoken against him.' These people are grumblers and faultfinders; they follow their own evil desires; they boast about themselves and flatter others for their own advantage" (Jude 1:14–16).[2] *The Lord was coming to judge – christ*

4. Enoch's walk with God put him in a place to receive inside information. Apply the following to us today: "When the Spirit of truth comes, he will guide you into all truth. He will not speak on his own but will tell you what he has heard. He will tell you about the future" (John 16:13 NLT).

5. How could Enoch's revelation have motivated him to seek God more fervently? *There will be a judgment Day.* *Wants to be Holy ones *

6. Believing there is future judgment for sinners and reward for those who walk with God changes how we live on earth. According to the following, what two actions will keep our walk pure on earth? "If then you have been raised with

Christ, seek the things that are above, where Christ is, seated at the right hand of God. Set your minds on things that are above, not on things that are on earth" (Col. 3:1–2 ESV).

also phil 4:6-7.   *1. seek Christ*
2. seek godly

7. How might walking with God have altered Enoch's attachment to earth? *cleave to God + not to things*
earthly

A Child Shall Lead Them

I wonder if the birth of Methuselah prompted Enoch to seek the Lord? If so, he's not alone. A dear friend in California had a similar experience when he cradled his firstborn son. How could those tiny fingers squeeze his thumb and heart at the same time? This fragile life depended on him for protection and direction in life. What would he tell him? A tremendous sense of responsibility thrust him into a search that led him to Jesus.

My Georgia relatives told me about another father impacted by his children. Psychology professor Rich Suplita was the advisor for the atheist club at the University of Georgia when he attended an event sponsored by Watkinsville First Baptist Church. Some of the church members suggested he read the gospel of John and reconsider biblical Christianity. Suplita did, and a few weeks later, he invited Christ into his life.

What strikes me the most in this story is that while Suplita had no problem telling his university students there was no God, he could not look his own children in the eye and say that. Suplita discovered the pleasure of walking with the Lord and now actively introduces others to Christ.

Adam was still alive when Enoch's son Methuselah was born. Perhaps Enoch had heard Adam recall the story of when God created Eve from his rib and the experience of naming all the animals. But Enoch didn't walk with God until he had a son to lead.

For Enoch and these two modern-day fathers, the responsibility of guiding their children caused them to reevaluate their lives. Perhaps the Holy Spirit impressed Jesus's warning on their hearts: "If anyone causes one of these little ones—those who believe in me—to stumble, it would be better for them if a large millstone were hung around their neck and they were thrown into the sea" (Mark 9:42). Finding God transformed their purpose and destinies. Have you considered who's watching you? Are you showing them how to walk with Jesus?

CLOSING PRAYER

Use this space to turn your insights and responses into prayers.

I Want to Remember . . .

Today's takeaways from #LittleFaithBigGod are:

Day Four

God Equips Us for Success

"I belong to my beloved, and his desire is for me."
—Song of Solomon 7:10

"Listen to what Jesus showed me," my friend Nan said. "When I come home, my little dog Eli wags his tail, whimpers in delight, and dances around my feet. He is so happy to see me. This week I realized that is how Jesus feels when I show up to spend time with him."

Wow! I had never pictured God getting excited because I made time for him. But Nan is right. Zephaniah 3:17 portrays God singing over his people. I see a mother twirling a child in her arms as she sings over her. Who doesn't want to spend time with someone who shows that kind of delight in her?

Perhaps you're thinking, "You don't know where I've been and what I've done. I'm no innocent babe. God couldn't feel that way about me."

Jesus covers that too. He told a story in which a rebellious son broke his father's rules and heart and squandered his inheritance (Luke 15:11–32). What do you think happened when this bedraggled prodigal returned home? His father dropped everything, raced to welcome him with a bear hug, and threw a lavish party to celebrate his son's homecoming.

Sometimes we think we have to clean up before we show up. The son just had to return home to enjoy his father's love. The father provided the best robe and a ring for his son's finger. Our Father wraps us in the robe of his righteousness (Isa. 61:10).

Walking with Jesus includes making time to connect with him. What starts as a discipline soon turns to delight. We don't want to miss our opportunity to be refreshed and discern God's leading. Before Enoch walked into heaven, he walked with God on earth. The Bible shows various ways for us to walk with the One who delights in us.

Scripture Reading..
GENESIS 5:24

Study and Reflection

1. The Bible says, "Enoch walked with God," instead of, "God walked with Enoch." God knows where he is going. He invites us to walk with him. In the following Scriptures, circle how we are to walk, and then explain what that would look like in your life and relationship with God.

   a. "So I say, walk by the Spirit, and you will not gratify the desires of the flesh." (Gal. 5:16).

   b. "I have no greater joy than to hear that my children are walking in the truth" (3 John 4).

   c. "Walk in the way of love, just as Christ loved us and gave himself up for us as a fragrant offering and sacrifice to God" (Eph. 5:2).

   d. "You were formerly darkness, but now you are Light in the Lord; walk as children of Light (Eph. 5:8 NASB).

   e. "Be careful how you walk, not as unwise men but as wise" (Eph. 5:15 NASB). *not by obstructing the truth but by wisdom.*

   f. "We walk by faith, not by sight" (2 Cor. 5:7 NASB).

g. "The one who says he abides in him [Jesus] ought himself to walk in the same manner as He walked" (1 John 2:6 NASB).

h. "Can two people walk together without agreeing on the direction?" (Amos 3:3 NLT).

2. John wrote that we could experience fellowship with the Father and the Son when we walk in the light. What do you learn about walking in the light from the following?

> My dear children, let's not just talk about love; let's practice real love. This is the only way we'll know we're living truly, living in God's reality. It's also the way to shut down debilitating self-criticism, even when there is something to it. For God is greater than our worried hearts and knows more about us than we do ourselves.
>
> And friends, once that's taken care of and we're no longer accusing or condemning ourselves, we're bold and free before God! We're able to stretch our hands out and receive what we asked for because we're doing what he said, doing what pleases him. Again, this is God's command: to believe in his personally named Son, Jesus Christ. He told us to love each other, in line with the original command. As we keep his commands, we live deeply and surely in him, and he lives in us. And this is how we experience his deep and abiding presence in us: by the Spirit he gave us. (1 John 3:18–24 MSG)

3. What applications do you draw from today's lesson?

Enoch Walked with God

Do you believe God wants the pleasure of your company? Enoch testifies to this. "It was by faith that Enoch was taken up to heaven without dying—'he disappeared, because God took him.' For before he was taken up, he was known as a person who pleased God" (Heb. 11:5 NLT).

Dutch Sheets writes, "What is for us 'the pleasure of *His* company,' can become for God 'the pleasure of *our* company.' For most, this is an unheard-of concept. It's one thing to believe God can use us. And believing that our obedience to His laws pleases Him? No problem. But I can't help but wonder how many people realize their presence can bring pleasure to the Lord."[3]

God created us to share life together and to enjoy our relationship with him like we would with a best friend. For example, think about your best friend. Why do you enjoy spending time with each other? Is it because of what they do for you? Or is it because of who they are? I bet it's the second. We hire people to serve us. But we can't buy true friendship.

Jesus wants to share life with you. In walking with him, we connect with his loving heart and receive comfort, warning, and insights (John 16:13–15). He revealed future events to Enoch that equipped him for his prophetic ministry (Jude 14–23).

How do we walk with the Lord and develop a friendship with someone who is perfect and invisible? The Bible offers some practical advice. We walk

- in the Spirit.
- in truth.

- in love.
- in light.
- in wisdom.
- by faith.
- as Jesus walked.
- in agreement with God.

Walking carries the idea of movement. God wants our company and has invited us to follow him. Here are some ways to keep in step.

Invest in Your Relationship

Jesus's disciple John referred to himself as the "one whom Jesus loved." Jesus loved all the disciples, but John enjoyed a special closeness with Jesus because he sought it. He personalized the love Christ had for all the disciples (1 John 4:16). We can too.

Close relationships require investments of time, not just the passing of time. For example, we enjoyed the Johnsons the year we were neighbors. We played games, painted trim, and shared confidences and Polly's pies together. Decades later, I still cherish hearing from them. Conversely, we've had other neighbors for decades, but, because we've only shared passing waves, we aren't close.

One evening after listening to my husband's rich thoughts, I realized how much I missed this aspect of him and how our busy lives were sabotaging our closeness. It's impossible to dive into the depths of the heart on the fly. Living, parenting, and ministering together were no substitutes for listening and sharing our souls with one another. We learned to schedule time for just the two of us.

Sermons and ministry activities don't replace one-on-one time with God either. It's important to practice his presence in daily life, but we also need regular times to personally relate to our Best Friend and bask in his company.

Trust Him in the Valley

Some believers stumble over adversity. They wonder if they've done something wrong or if God has left them. They assumed a walk with Jesus would be a garden stroll. But poison ivy and yellow jackets (and in one case a talking serpent) lurk in gardens. Jesus said to expect trouble in this world, but in him we can have peace (John 16:33). With the number of years Enoch accumulated, I'm sure he passed through some rough spots.

God doesn't forsake us when our path leads us through dark valleys. With the psalmist we can declare, "Even though I walk through the darkest valley, I will fear no evil, for you are with me; your rod and your staff, they comfort me" (Ps. 23:4). When night descends, we need only to whisper his name and we will have light (Ps. 139:12).

Get Up after a Stumble

We all stumble in many ways, but our trips aren't fatal, because the Lord holds our hand. (Ps. 37:24). The psalmist asked God to "Point out anything you find in me that makes you sad, and lead me along the path of everlasting life" (Ps. 139:24 TLB).

The following passage describes the fellowship we enjoy with the triune God when we walk in the light. Confession restores us after a misstep.

> If we claim to have fellowship with him and yet walk in the darkness, we lie and do not live out the truth. But if we walk in the light, as he is in the light, we have fellowship with one another, and the blood of Jesus, his Son, purifies us from all sin.
>
> If we claim to be without sin, we deceive ourselves and the truth is not in us. If we confess our sins, he is

faithful and just and will forgive us our sins and purify us from all unrighteousness. (1 John 1:6–9)

To confess our sins means to agree with what God says about them. We agree that our sin is destructive and falls short of his glory (James 1:15; Rom. 3:23). We also agree that because we are in Christ, our sins are forgiven (Heb. 10:22 NLT).

Anne Graham Lotz said, "We come back to the cross, not for forgiveness since we are already forgiven, but to confess our sin and be cleansed that we might maintain a right fellowship with God and with others and ourselves."[4]

"Let us go right into the presence of God with sincere hearts fully trusting him. For our guilty consciences have been sprinkled with Christ's blood to make us clean" (Heb. 10:22 NLT).

When we walk in agreement with God, we stop making excuses for our blunders or blaming our circumstances and other people; instead we concur with his assessment of our actions and attitudes. For example, "You're right, Lord. I've let fear, not faith, control me. I'm sorry. Thanks for getting me back on track."

It is as important to confess our cleansing as it is to confess our wrongs—especially when we have a hard time forgiving ourselves. When we confess our sin to God, we are affirming equally that what he calls sin is wrong and that the one he calls clean is clean.[5]

Walking by Faith Takes Practice

Have you ever watched a child learn to walk? At first, toddlers fall every few steps. They cling to furniture and adult legs for support. Parents don't scold their children for falling. They cheer them for trying. Soon, the falls pay off. They are scampering around freely.

Our heavenly Father applauds our efforts to walk by faith. He's counting our steps, not our stumbles. Learning to walk by faith is a process too. Enjoy it! Your desire and effort delight our Father.

CLOSING PRAYER

Ask God to help you grow in the area(s) you identified today.

I Want to Remember . . .

Today's takeaways from #LittleFaithBigGod are:

Day Five
God Will Take You Home

"By faith Enoch was taken from this life."
—Hebrews 11:5

Imagine unwinding with God at the end of the day. You've shared your thoughts, concerns, and joys, and enjoyed just being together. The earth smells fresher and cleaner than you remember. The corals and pinks of the sky are more brilliant. "Wait, where are we?" you ask.

"I'm taking you home with me today," God says.

While we don't know the particulars, something like that happened to Enoch. His miraculous departure foreshadows a future event for the church. Could we be the generation that skips death?

Scripture Reading...
1 THESSALONIANS 4:15–17

Study and Reflection

1. We've already seen that God gave Enoch a special revelation concerning still future events. Enoch's departure from this life is also a precursor of an event that many call the rapture of the saints. How might the future church's experience resemble Enoch's? "According to the Lord's word, we tell you that we who are still alive, who are left until the coming of the Lord, will certainly not precede those who have fallen asleep. For the Lord himself will come down from heaven, with a loud command, with the voice of the archangel and with the trumpet call of God, and the dead in Christ will rise first. After that, we who are still alive and are left will be caught up together with them in the clouds to meet the Lord in the air. And so we will be with the Lord forever" (1 Thess. 4:15–17).

2. Why is the second coming of Jesus a wonderful hope for those who walk with God? "But let me reveal to you a wonderful secret. We will not all die, but we will all be transformed! It will happen in a moment, in the blink of an eye, when the last trumpet is blown. For when the trumpet sounds, those who have died will be raised to live forever. And we who are living will also be transformed. For our dying bodies must be transformed into bodies that will never die; our mortal bodies must be transformed into immortal bodies" (1 Cor. 15:51–53 NLT).

3. What will the earth be like close to Christ's return? "You must understand this: In the last days there will be violent

periods of time. People will be selfish and love money. They will brag, be arrogant, and use abusive language. They will curse their parents, show no gratitude, have no respect for what is holy, and lack normal affection for their families. They will refuse to make peace with anyone. They will be slanderous, lack self-control, be brutal, and have no love for what is good" (2 Tim. 3:1–3 GWT).

4. If you knew the Lord was returning today, would you be ready? If not, what do you need to change in order to be ready? *Less things to do!*

Walking into Heaven

We won't all die. Yep, you read that right. God deals with us individually. Abel and Enoch both pleased God. Both entered heaven. Yet one was murdered and the other escaped death.

When Jesus told Peter how he would die, Peter asked about John. Jesus answered, "If I want him to remain until I come, what is that to you? You follow Me!" (John 21:22 NASB). God's grace is sufficient for what he's laid out for each of us.

The second coming that Enoch foretold remains on the horizon. Prophecy is a shadow, not a photograph. Before prophecies come to pass, their details remain vague. Afterward, we see how the fulfillment matches the prediction. Some Old Testament Scriptures contain prophecies concerning the first and second coming of Christ in the same verse. God gives us enough information to recognize nothing happens by chance and to know he is carrying out his eternal plan. What is clear is that Jesus will return for his church.

Jesus asked this haunting question, "When the Son of Man comes, will he find faith on the earth?" (Luke 18:8). Those who faithfully walk with the Lord and are faithful to his call have nothing to fear (Matt. 24:45–51). In light of Scripture, watching the times should motivate us to stay in step with our Lord, as Enoch did.

Before the Lord returns to execute judgment, he has promised to take those who've faithfully walked with him straight to heaven. If we're alive at that time, like Enoch, we will skip death (1 Thess. 4:17). But whether we enter through death or by rapture, Jesus is big enough to guide us safely home.

CLOSING PRAYER

Use this space to turn your insights and responses into prayers.

I Want to Remember . . .

Today's takeaways from #LittleFaithBigGod are:

Prayer Requests

How to Grow a Hero's Faith in a Hostile World

Noah means "rest."

The animals gathered in pairs and trotted onto the ark as if drawn by a call only they could hear. Noah waved his hand under his nose and chuckled when he ushered in the pair of pigs. Surely his neighbors would believe now.

But not one budged. Noah's heart felt heavier than the logs he'd hoisted to build the ark. How many times had he pleaded with them to believe and join him on the ark? With a thud, God honored their choices and sealed the door—and their fates.

HAVE YOU EVER LOOKED AT THE CONDITION OF OUR WORLD and wondered how your children and grandchildren can walk with God when they are surrounded by so many evil influences? Let Noah's story encourage you. He practiced righteous faith in an age of complete depravity. And Noah believed God would save his loved ones if he followed God's instructions.

We've seen that faith is "the conviction of things not seen" (Heb. 11:1). Noah demonstrated faith when he "obeyed God, who warned him about things that had never happened before" (Heb. 11:7 NLT). When the Lord told Noah to build an ark, Noah followed God's instructions, even though he likely had never experienced rain, much less a flood. Noah's awe of God overrode any argument his senses or neighbors raised. In reverence, he hammered amid scoffs and preached to an unreceptive audience.

His genuine faith caused him to bow to what must have seemed an outlandish plan. The Bible calls this the "obedience that comes from faith" (Rom. 16:26). Jesus said: "Those who accept my commandments and obey them are the ones who love me. And because they love me, my Father will love them. And I will love them and reveal myself to each of them" (John 14:21 NLT). God responded to Noah's faithfulness and rescued him and his family in a most unusual way.

Day One
Noah Made God the Boss

Experts believe a simple seatbelt would have saved Princess Diana the night of her fatal crash. In *The Day Diana Died*, a friend of Princess Diana's said Dodi Fayed made the princess feel safe. Is that why she didn't buckle up?

Some trust their hunches; one friend believes in science while another believes our political system will protect us. Our faith is only as reliable as its object. Misdirected faith—no matter how sincere or strong—eventually disappoints. Even worse, it can destroy us.

The people in Noah's day trusted their experiences and pooh-poohed Noah's warning. They believed life would continue as usual. They planned weddings and business ventures without thought of pending doom.

But Noah was different. He walked with God and, like Enoch, received a warning for the future.

Feelings, people, and institutions can disappoint us. But Jesus never fails. Making him the Lord of our lives protects us and simplifies life. When we run our decisions by him, criticism and fears lose their power over us. We know we're in step with the One who writes history.

Scripture Reading...

GENESIS 6:5–8:22

Study and Reflection

1. Record your observations from Noah's story in Genesis.

   ① Unimaginable ② Noah was obedient ③ thunder rained for 40 days. ④ Lord shut him in. ⑤ Dove + Olive Brand (peace)

2. What similarities do you see between Noah and Enoch?

   Obey / obediance / good heart

3. What lessons do you draw from Noah?

   he did something that there was no precidence for, no history rain.

4. What personal applications do you find in the story of the ark? *① Obey God, love Dale – no light @ the end of that tunnel – Just need to love him*

Noah, a Man of Persevering Faith

When Noah heard God's warning, he had never seen a raindrop, let alone a flood. When he cut the first log, could he imagine a floating monstrosity that would hold his family and all those animals? It doesn't matter if Noah could envision it or not. He only had to follow God's directions. Faith is demonstrated in obedience, not in imagination (James 2:20).

Persevering Faith

Noah was 500 years old when Shem was born (Gen. 5:32) and 600 years old when the flood came (Gen. 7:6). If he worked on the ark for 120 years as some theologians believe (Gen. 6:3; 1 Pet. 3:20), he started building it 20 years before his sons were born. Who helped him when he started? If he hired help, they must not have believed in the project. He had only the support of his wife. At least we hope she supported him. It may have taken her time to get on board—pun intended. Faith is demonstrated in perseverance.

Making Jesus our Lord or boss brings clarity but doesn't completely eliminate stress from our lives. Sometimes his directions conflict with human understanding, like investing more in his kingdom than in our retirement, taking a lower paying job so we can spend more time with our family or ministry, or moving to a dangerous part of the world when we're content in our cozy cul-de-sac. We honor God through our actions. When we trust God's promises and heed his warnings, then, like Noah, we discover the path to righteousness to be evident even in a dark world.

God forewarned Noah about the flood and instructed him on how to save his family and whoever would join them. God has warned us that judgment follows death and, like in the days of Noah, destruction is coming to the earth. He has also told us how to be delivered.

As Noah built and boarded the ship according to God's instructions, so we too must anchor our faith in Christ and follow his guidelines for life. Doing so will save us from the undertow of evil and pending destruction.

CLOSING PRAYER

Use this space to turn your insights and responses into prayers.

I Want to Remember . . .

Today's takeaways from #LittleFaithBigGod are:

Day Two
Noah Obeyed God's Call

Author Barbara Johnson once described a cartoon she'd seen about Noah: "The little man and his animals were gathered around a big sign near a gate that said, 'Noah's Park.' The voice coming down from above said something like, 'OK, now, let's try it again. And this time listen carefully!'"[6]

Noah was probably a farmer, not a carpenter. Because of his profession, it would have made sense for God to ask him to build a park. Has God ever asked you to do something out of your skill set? Thankfully, Noah heeded God's outlandish call and pursued a venture he would not otherwise have attempted.

Noah's obedience accomplished more than he could have imagined. We're here today because Noah believed and obeyed God. I doubt Noah dreamed anyone would be reading his story thousands of years later. His faith in a big God brought salvation to many, whereas the smug self-reliance of the majority destroyed them.

Do you feel inadequate for the task God has set before you? God equips those he calls when they rely on him.

Scripture Reading...
GENESIS 6:5–22
HEBREWS 11:7

Study and Reflection

1. Faith acts in response to God's initiative. God warned Noah about something Noah had never seen.

   a. According to Hebrews 11:7, how did Noah express his faith? *Holy fear, condemned the world.*

   b. What do you learn about faith from Noah's example? *faith was action*

2. Have you ever been in a group of people whose coarse jokes, language, and lifestyle mocked your faith and values? Imagine every person in the whole world being that way. Contrast Noah (Gen. 6:8–9) with the culture in which he lived (Gen. 6:5, 11–13).

3. What warning and promise did God give Noah (Gen. 6:17–21)? *Do as I say + you will be saved.*

4. Noah faithfully walked with God before he announced the flood. God used Noah's obedience to save his family during this catastrophic event (Gen. 8:18–19). What warning and promise do you find in the following, and what role does

obedience play for us in our everyday lives? "Today I have given you the choice between life and death, between blessings and curses. Now I call on heaven and earth to witness the choice you make. Oh, that you would choose life, so that you and your descendants might live! You can make this choice by loving the LORD your God, obeying him, and committing yourself firmly to him. This is the key to your life" (Deut. 30:19–20 NLT).

5. "In reverence [Noah] prepared an ark for the salvation of his household" (Heb. 11:7 NASB). Noah turned everyday work into service for God. What would it look like for you to do your work in reverence, based on the following passages?

   a. "And whatever you do, whether in word or deed, do it all in the name of the Lord Jesus, giving thanks to God the Father through him" (Col. 3:17).

   b. "Better is one day in your courts than a thousand elsewhere; I would rather be a doorkeeper in the house of my God than dwell in the tents of the wicked" (Ps. 84:10).

6. Faith provides assurance of what we hope for.

   a. In response to God's promise, what did Noah hope for when he built and boarded the ark (Heb. 11:1, 7; Gen. 6:17–21)? His family would live

b. What hope keeps you persevering in the role God has
   given you? *my family will not perish. yet*
   if they follow evil ways they will.

Faith Changes How We Work

If you were Noah, what would you have hoped for as you water-
proofed the ark with tar (Heb. 11:1)? Would you be hoping your
work would hold and that life would improve after the flood?

Noah must have felt weary at times during the long years he
worked on the ark and preached. What kept him preaching when
no one believed his message? Paul understood discouragement.
He wrote, "So let's not get tired of doing what is good. At just the
right time we will reap a harvest of blessing if we don't give up"
(Gal. 6:9 NLT). *(that my family will turn to live)*
Noah trusted the Lord to reward his labor and, at the very least,
save him, his extended family, and some animals. He hammered
logs to secure his family and humankind's future.

When we do God's will in the power of the Holy Spirit, our
work is never wasted. Even if we don't see the results we pictured,
if we don't give up, a blessing will come. But half of an ark would
not have saved anyone.

Noah couldn't save the world, but he rescued his family—and
us. God created us to do good works too (Eph. 2:10). And like
Noah, we may not see the ripple effect in our lifetime. We glorify
him when we heed his call, through his power (Eph. 5:18). Gutting
out our labor in our own strength, or for human approval, breeds
resentment and bruises people. We take on tasks God never meant
for us to do. This exhausts us and robs others of the roles God
planned for them.

Faith, not busyness or religious activity, produces fruitfulness.
The religious teachers in Jesus's day prayed and preached out of

selfish motives. Noah hammered and sawed out of reverence for God.

Whether we're negotiating a business deal, changing a diaper, or teaching a class, working with excellence as unto the Lord turns work into worship. Working as unto the Lord alters how we do business. Getting the best deal won't be a triumph if it robs the car dealer's family of an honest wage. Taking on that valuable client will bring eternal loss if it takes me away from the God-given work of training my children.

Ultimately, God is looking for worshippers. Work generated from faith transforms mundane tasks into worship. Caring for a sick child becomes an opportunity to show him he's valuable. Knowing he's valuable, even when he's sick, has the power to change how he views himself and other people.

Noah's preaching didn't rescue many lives, but it pleased God, earned him eternal rewards, and saved future generations. It's better to focus on whom we serve than what we accomplish. Only God knows the lasting fruit our work will bear.

God showed a humble farmer how to build an ark to save his family. What has God called you to do to help rescue your family and community? *Live Bold, show loving kindness sacrifice for my family ?*

CLOSING PRAYER

Use this space to turn your insights and responses into prayers.

I Want to Remember . . .

Today's takeaways from #LittleFaithBigGod are:

Day Three

Noah Trusted God with the Hard Stuff

One of my friends directs a ministry that rescues vulnerable children around the world. It is inconceivable to think there are people who sell the virginity of their orphaned relatives or use them as slaves.

Those tiny glimpses into the world of exploitation puncture my heart. What must God suffer with these children every day? While some wonder how he could destroy the world in Noah's day, I hear my friend's stories and wonder why he lets the human race continue.

The opening paragraphs of Genesis chapter 6 set the stage for God's judgment during Noah's time. Scholars differ over who the "sons of God" were. Author J. Vernon McGee says that he doesn't believe demons would be called sons of God and that good angels wouldn't be involved in something wicked. Since Genesis is a book of genealogies, he thinks the sons of God refer to Adam's godly line through his son Seth. They intermarried with the daughters of men from the wicked line of Cain.[7]

Others think this could refer to ungodly powerful rulers. "The point of this cryptic passage, whichever way we take it, is that a new stage has been reached in the progress of evil, with God's bounds overstepped in yet another realm."[8]

The multiplication of wickedness corrupted and filled the earth with such violence that God regretted creating the human race. Without the companionship of others who shared his faith, Noah walked faithfully with God.

Scripture Reading..

GENESIS 6:5–7:1; 9:1, 6–24
HEBREWS 11:7

Study and Reflection

1. How did Noah demonstrate remarkable faith in his time (Gen. 6:5–7:1)? What does this show you about faith?

   [handwritten] obtn, built the ark. Followed gods step by step instructn

2. "By his faith Noah condemned the rest of the world" (Heb. 11:7). How did Noah's faith condemn the rest of the world?

   [handwritten] He just went the opposite way.

3. Noah had to trust God's judgments, timing, and provision for this huge assignment. What part of your work stresses you? How can you trust God with your challenge?

   [handwritten] not work, marriage; Dale's negativity + arrogance —

4. Have you ever wondered how people can be "prolife" and support capital punishment? Do these ideas seem contradictory? These positions are based on Genesis 9:5–6. God gave this command before the Mosaic Law. Whatever side you come down on, consider the reason why God required the life of animals and people who murder human beings and share your thoughts. "And I will require the blood of anyone who takes another person's life. If a wild animal kills a person, it must die. And anyone who murders a fellow human must die. If anyone takes a human life, that person's life will also be taken by human hands. For God made human beings in his own image" (NLT). (See Romans 13:3–4 for a New Testament view on the government's role in this.)

   [handwritten] I have a problem w/ this. New testament. love turn the oth cheek. all life is sacred.

Between God & each.

Rainbow / sign of the covenant

5. Our culture has hijacked the true significance of the rainbow. What is the rainbow's real meaning (Gen. 9:8–17)?

There will be rain after the drought?

6. How did Noah show himself to be an ordinary man after the flood (Gen. 9:20–29)? *He got drunk.*

7. What did you learn about God from Noah's story?

He's all powerful, he does speak to us.

How Did Noah Feed All of Those Animals?

One Easter season, my young children adopted a downy chick and baby duck from a farm supply store. Brant dubbed his duck Jordan. She bonded with Brant like a baby with its mother and entertained us with comedic splashes into a plastic kiddie pool.

Ginny's chick Rosie grew into an independent Road Island Red. Rosie and Jordan scrounged for snacks together. Sometimes they'd mosey over to our neighbor's house and peck their back door for Cheerios. Our backyard neighbor nicknamed them Poncho and Cisco.

My husband, Larry, built a pen for their nighttime protection. Unlike children, Jordan and Rosie bedded down without prompting. After Jordan outgrew the kiddie pool, we tried to release her at a friend's pond where other ducks lived. We said our good-byes and turned to leave, but she clung to us like static electricity. We brought her home.

One morning, Jordan didn't move. Heartbroken, I sat on my daughter's white iron bed with an arm around each of my sorrowing children. From the window, we watched Larry, slumped shouldered, shovel a grave. We all grieved the loss of our funny friend.

While I watched, a movement behind Larry attracted me. A white head popped up from Jordan's crate. Jordan climbed out of the box and started pecking at the ground behind Larry! Laughter choked my speech. I knocked on the window. Larry frowned, not appreciating my amusement.

"Behind you," I pointed. "Look behind you!"

At that moment, Jordan zipped past Larry like Road Runner pursued by Wile E. Coyote. She sped circles around the yard, flapping and quacking. "I'm alive! I'm alive!" she seemed to say.

A friend and vet explained Jordan had been in hibernation, a coma-like sleep that doesn't require food or drink. Jordan gave me a glimpse of what Noah must have experienced on the ark. How else could he have stored enough food for all those animals for a year? Hibernation would have kept the animals from being restless and from needing much food, care, and exercise.

Jordan and Rosie helped me understand Jesus wasn't exaggerating when he said a sparrow couldn't drop to the ground without his Father knowing it. God has given each creature a unique personality.

The Bible says, "When sin is allowed to grow, it gives birth to death" (James 1:15 NLT). In Noah's time, wickedness brought judgment to the whole earth. God's tears must have mingled with the rain when he watched people and animals that bore his thumbprint drown because of humankind's violence. The rainbow is a reminder of his covenant and love for all creatures.

CLOSING PRAYER

Use this space to turn your insights and responses into prayers.

I Want to Remember . . .

Today's takeaways from #LittleFaithBigGod are:

Noah Trusted God's Decisions

If after 120 years of peddling your product the only people who bought it were your immediate family, would you consider yourself a failure? Would you question your endeavor? Would you doubt yourself or your assignment?

At one point in his ministry, my husband counseled inner-city children at a group home in Durham, North Carolina, one day a week. And just when Larry thought he was making progress, a child would spend a weekend at home and witness a murder. Perhaps more damaging was how the children's parents repeatedly reneged on their promises.

"I'm getting a bicycle this weekend," one boy beamed. Larry braced himself, knowing next week this boy would return crestfallen. Was Larry making any difference in the lives of these children?

A receptive audience gives back. Rejection, whether caused by callousness or disillusionment, drains energy. Imagine never having one positive response to your message.

Noah walked with God during the most corrupt era in history. He faithfully preached to his culture even when no one responded. His faith condemned the world by showing it was possible to please God and escape his wrath. His generation could never say, "We didn't know."

A young man of Athens once told Socrates, "I hate you, because every time I meet you, you show me what I am."[9] Preaching repentance to obstinate people must have wearied Noah more than building the ark. Noah was God's mouthpiece. In rejecting him, the people flaunted their hatred for God.

Noah fulfilled his God-given purpose. But if he measured his worth by the number of converts his preaching had won, then Noah would have considered himself a failure. But Noah—and Larry—did not fail. Their obedience delighted God and fulfilled his purpose. Some fruit can't be measured in a lifetime.

Scripture Reading...
Continue Genesis 6:5–9:29

Study and Reflection

1. One year, vandals broke into our ministry office, shook up soft drinks, and sprayed them over bookcases, files, and walls. We rescued what we could, but threw out many books and files because of the sticky residue. During Noah's lifetime, "every inclination of the thoughts of the human heart was only evil all the time" and the earth was "full of violence" (Gen. 6:5, 11–13). How would you feel watching the people you created willfully destroy each other and ruin your beautiful creation? How did God feel when he saw how man's great wickedness had covered the earth (Gen. 6:6)?

   Sdd + hanitud

2. How does sin affect God today? Consider this question based on the following verses of Scripture.

   a. "And do not bring sorrow to God's Holy Spirit by the way you live" (Eph. 4:30 NLT).

   b. "God is a righteous judge, And a God who has indignation every day" (Ps. 7:11 NASB)

3. Who suffered because of human sin? *god + man.*

4. Noah walked with God in spite of his godless culture. How does this encourage you? *Continue, do not look to others + the world.*

5. Most of us find it easier to mention Jesus to people we think will be receptive than to scoffers. An occasional positive response keeps us going. Noah was called "a preacher of righteousness" (2 Pet. 2:5 NASB). Considering Noah's audience, what does this tell you about Noah? *persistent.*

A Cranky Old Man?

While cartoons portray God as a cranky, wild-haired man hurling lightning bolts from the sky, the Bible paints a different picture.

- God warned Adam that eating from the tree of the knowledge of good and evil would bring death. *wise.*

- God warned Cain that sin was crouching like a panther ready to pounce and destroy him.
- God sent Enoch and Noah to warn their generations of coming judgment.

Yet, despite all this, his warnings were scorned and ignored. Throughout history, those whom God wanted to rescue abused and killed his messengers. When we see history from God's perspective, his continued patience amazes those of us who struggle to forgive one repeated offense.

Noah was born sixty-nine years after Enoch was no more. If Noah's generation wouldn't repent after centuries of warnings, do you think another ten or twenty years would have made a difference? Even today, it is God's patience and unwillingness for any to perish that delays Christ's return.

God took Enoch from a world that was becoming increasingly wicked. God left Noah and removed everyone else from a world that had become completely wicked. These events serve as both warnings and sources of encouragement for our generation. Judgment is coming. But God has provided an ark. *Christ is the ark.*

CLOSING PRAYER

Use this space to turn your insights and responses into prayers.

I Want to Remember . . .

Today's takeaways from #LittleFaithBigGod are:

Day Five
Noah Trusted God's Foreknowledge

God prefers to save life. He gave the rainbow as a sign of the everlasting covenant he made with every living creature never to destroy all life again by flood. The Bible says, "For God did not send his Son into the world to condemn the world, but to save the world through him. Whoever believes in him is not condemned, but whoever does not believe stands condemned already because they have not believed in the name of God's one and only Son" (John 3:17–18).

Jesus is the ark that saves us from eternal death and judgment. He said, "I am the resurrection and the life; he who believes in Me will live even if he dies" (John 11:25 NASB).

People in Noah's day saw the huge boat. They heard Noah's warning and invitation. Even after Noah's family boarded the ark, God waited seven days before the first raindrop fell (Gen. 7:4, 10).

When I hear about a dangerous rescue, I think of my firefighter friends. How tragic it is when a noble person loses life or limb saving someone who intentionally disregarded safety warnings and restraints. How wicked it would be if those rescued mocked the one who died to save them. Those who spurn God's way of salvation show disdain for the One who gave his life to rescue them.

Scripture Reading..
CONTINUE GENESIS 6:5–9:29

Study and Reflection

1. Peter wrote, "God waited patiently in the days of Noah while the ark was being built. In it only a few people, eight in all,

were saved through water" (1 Pet. 3:20). What does this tell you about God? *only a few will be saved.*

2. Relate the days of Noah to God's future judgment. "The Lord is not slow in keeping his promise, as some understand slowness. Instead he is patient with you, not wanting anyone to perish, but everyone to come to repentance. But the day of the Lord will come like a thief. The heavens will disappear with a roar; the elements will be destroyed by fire, and the earth and everything done in it will be laid bare. Since everything will be destroyed in this way, what kind of people ought you to be? You ought to live holy and godly lives as you look forward to the day of God and speed its coming. That day will bring about the destruction of the heavens by fire, and the elements will melt in the heat. But in keeping with his promise we are looking forward to a new heaven and a new earth, where righteousness dwells" (2 Pet. 3:9–13).

3. How did Jesus relate his return to the days of Noah? Base your response on the following:

"As it was in the days of Noah, so it will be at the coming of the Son of Man. For in the days before the flood, people were eating and drinking, marrying and giving in marriage, up to the day Noah entered the ark; and they knew nothing about what would happen until the flood came and took them all away. That is how it will be at the coming of the Son of Man. Two men will be in the field; one will be taken and the other left. Two women will be grinding with a hand mill; one will be taken and the other left.

"Therefore keep watch, because you do not know on what day your Lord will come. But understand this: If the owner of the house had known at what time of night the thief was coming, he would have kept watch and would not have let his house be broken into. So you also must be ready, because the Son of Man will come at an hour when you do not expect him" (Matt. 24:37–44).

Trust + obey.

4. How do these warnings apply to us?

Trust + obey.

5. What impressed you most about Noah's story?

obedience. Trust.

A Judge or a Savior?

God closed the ark door, and the destinies of those on and off the boat were decided—according to their choices. Indecision is a decision. The Scripture says, "Now is the day of salvation" (2 Cor. 6:2). Have you responded to God's invitation? No one knows when the door of opportunity will slam shut.

The flood waters divided humankind into two groups—those on the ark and those off, the saved and the condemned. Noah's drunkenness and immodesty show an imperfect man. As one gal in my Bible study said, "Noah got drunk, Noah got naked, and Noah got mad." But the Lord counted him as righteous because of his faith (Rom. 4:5; Gen. 9:20–21).

The New Testament divides people into two groups, too. Jesus used sheep and goats and wheat and chaff to illustrate the different natures of the two. The Bible calls believers saints and unbelievers sinners. Dr. Neil Anderson explains:

> Being a saint does not necessarily reflect any present measure of growth in character, but it does identify those who are rightly related to God. In the *King James Version* of the Bible, believers are called "saints," "holy ones" or "righteous ones" more than 240 times. In contrast, unbelievers are called "sinners" more than 330 times. Clearly the term "saint" is used in Scripture to refer to the believer, and "sinner" is used in reference to the unbeliever.[10]

After the flood, God drastically shortened the human life-span. Perhaps mercy motivated him to reduce the time evil people have to hone their wickedness. Extra years don't tend to soften hearts toward God. A poll by the National Association of Evangelicals (NAE) shows 63 percent of people accept Jesus as Lord and Savior between the ages of 4–14. This is commonly called the 4/14 window. The more we age, the less likely we are to be receptive to the gospel.[11]

As the ark clearly delineated two groups, so does the cross of Christ. God will separate the sheep from the goats and the wheat from the chaff (Matt. 13:30; 25:31–46). Judgment will show who chose Jesus and who chose the world.

Enoch depicts the rapture of believers. Noah reminds us of coming judgment. The coming of the Son of Man will be just like the days of Noah (Matt. 24:37–39). It's time to board our ark. "Whoever comes to me I will never drive away" (John 6:37). One day we will see Jesus. Today, we decide whether we will meet him as our Savior or as our Judge.

CLOSING PRAYER

Use this space to turn your insights and responses into prayers.

I Want to Remember . . .

Today's takeaways from #LittleFaithBigGod are:

Prayer Requests

Jesus Picked You to Be His Friend

Abraham means "father of a multitude."

Sarai stared at what had been their comfortable home. The wistful look in her beautiful eyes squeezed Abraham's heart. Behind them, a donkey grunted and stomped. "It will be all right," Abraham whispered in her ear, catching the lavender scent of her hair. Taking her elbow in one hand, he reached with his other hand to shut the door.

HEBREWS 11 SAYS MORE ABOUT ABRAHAM THAN ANYONE else. In Acts 7:1–8, Stephen used Abraham as a witness against the Pharisees. What did Abraham do to earn so much recognition?

James 2:23 says, "'Abraham believed God, and it was credited to him as righteousness,' and he was called God's friend." It's one thing to say I know a famous celebrity. It is quite another for that celebrity to call me her friend. The Bible calls Abraham God's friend, and Jesus calls believers his friends.

Companionship grows through shared experiences. God called Abraham on an adventure of faith, but he also called him into an eternal friendship.

God found Abraham in a pagan land and told him to leave his country and relatives. God would direct his steps. Abraham believed his Friend and left home without knowing where he was going.

Being someone who likes to know where I'm headed, I appreciate Abraham's example. In a time of transition, God told me to leave counseling but didn't make it clear where I was going. My joy faltered every time I *tried* to figure it out. Peace returned whenever I *trusted him* to lead me.

Abraham focused more on following his Friend than on figuring out the destination. Let's learn from his example.

Day One
God's Friends Trust Him

"How can you leave?" my friend from church asked as she wrapped another plate in tissue paper. "My husband and I believe God wants us in overseas missions, but we're not ready."

I looked at the boxes of kitchen items separated into "move" and "store" piles and remembered the miraculous way God had provided this California ranch that was close to our thriving church and ministry obligations. The storybook charm of the cedar shake roof and manicured lawn had captivated me at first sight. It was much more than we could have ever imagined owning in this high-priced housing area.

The mild climate and fenced-in backyard provided an ideal setting to raise two curious preschoolers. Our fruit trees supplied more apricots, plums, and pomegranates than we could eat. But God was nudging us away from our current ministry with youth into a new direction. Following his lead meant leaving the bounty of sunny California so my husband could attend seminary just below the Snowbelt in isolated Wynona Lake, Indiana. I guess our decision looked foolish.

Yet God had stirred our hearts on a mission trip to Poland. A radio series on spiritual gifts affirmed our restlessness. As we sought God, our hearts thumped with excitement.

Besides, God had called—*how could we not go?*

Larry and I had a young family when God launched us in a new direction. Our friends Ralph and LuElla were empty nesters when God called them to Egypt. Ralph emailed: "Twenty-four hours ago there was a bombing in Alexandria, Egypt, the city LuElla and I currently call home. . . . You might ask why are we here, why did we walk away from incredible friends, a home, community, family and meaningful work to come here? The answer to that question, asked by our Egyptian friends as well, is simply we listened to what God wanted from us and we obeyed."

Is that how Abraham felt when God called him to leave the thriving metropolis of Ur for a place he did not know? Ur was located in Mesopotamia, or modern-day Iraq, and was one of the most important cities of the ancient world. Did Sarah jump on board, or did Abraham have to convince her that God had spoken? Leaving security for the unknown must have looked foolish to their friends too. But God had called. What else could they do? God's friends follow his directions (John 14:15).

Scripture Reading...

Hebrews 11:8
Genesis 11:27–12:1

Study and Reflection

1. Abraham came from a family that worshipped false gods.
   "This is what the Lord, the God of Israel, says: Long ago your ancestors, including Terah, the father of Abraham and Nahor,

lived beyond the Euphrates River, and they worshipped other gods. But I took your ancestor Abraham from the land beyond the Euphrates and led him into the land of Canaan. I gave him many descendants through his son Isaac" (Josh. 24:2–3 NLT).

a. Who initiated the relationship between God and Abraham?

b. Who initiates the relationship between God and us? Jesus said, "You didn't choose me. I chose you" (John 15:16 NLT).

c. How have you experienced this in your own life?

2. My husband and I knew God had called us to leave a church we'd been a part of for more than a decade. I'd prayed he would call us *to* something before he called us *from* something. But God only partially answered my request. Sometimes he separates us from certain things so he can separate us to himself.

a. What did Abraham have to leave in order to walk with God (Gen. 12:1)?

b. Jesus told fishermen Peter, James, and John to leave their nets and follow him. No matter what he calls us from, he always calls us to himself. How do you apply this to your walk with the Lord?

3. Hebrews 11:8 commends Abraham's faith by saying he obeyed and went "without knowing where he was going." How is this related to faith as described in Hebrews 11:1–2?

4. Jesus said, "Why do you call me, 'Lord, Lord,' and do not do what I say?" (Luke 6:46). Has God called you to leave something familiar without showing you clearly where you are going? How does Abraham's story speak to you, especially in relationship to trusting God with the unseen?

When God Calls

You might think it never rains on those who obey God's call. But that was not true for Abraham, our friends, or us. Abraham and Sarah traded the comforts of home and familiarity of family to live in tents in a foreign culture. Their trek included burying their father, decades of infertility, and a rift with their nephew. Abraham had to send one son away and offer the other as a sacrifice.

Abraham's friendship with God held him steady through these confusing and painful dips. In fact, it was during the hard times that the roots of Abraham's faith dug deeper into God's character.

Larry and I lived in four states in four years. Most of our belongings laid in inaccessible storage during that time. We buried both of our fathers. When I learned a relative was going after the small inheritance my father had left us, I felt like a squashed grape. Ironically, our experience taught us the company of God on a rough road is better than a comfortable life outside his will.

Years later, I learned that the friend who'd helped me pack had split with her husband. Even more heartbreaking, they had married others from our Sunday school class who'd also divorced after we had left. I didn't know the circumstances, but I remembered how they had rejected what she'd called a clear assignment from God. I don't know what would have happened if she and her husband had left the familiar to follow God's lead. Neither do I know why Larry and I received the grace to go. I do know it's always better to stay in step with God than to play it safe.

When God spoke, Abraham trusted his Friend. What else could he do but obey his Lord?

CLOSING PRAYER

Use this space to turn your insights and responses into prayers.

I Want to Remember . . .

What do you want to remember from today's study? Let's encourage each other by sharing our takeaways on social media with the hashtag #LittleFaithBigGod.

Day Two

God's Friends Follow His Lead

*"Who I am becoming is much more important
than what I am doing."*
—Henry David Thoreau

Clear, measurable goals with time limits may enhance productivity, but I've found my goals don't always match God's plans for my life. God's more concerned with what he is accomplishing in me than what I'm achieving. His goal is to teach me to trust him.

God gave Abraham spectacular promises, but he didn't fill in such specifics as when, where, and how—until decades later. The Bible says God's Word "is a lamp for my feet, a light on my path" (Ps. 119:105). Someone carrying a lantern or torch in the dark can see only one or two steps ahead. The next step isn't revealed until we take the one lit before us (Prov. 4:18).

God may burn a vision in our hearts and leave the specifics fuzzy. If God laid out all of the details, I'd probably rely on the plan instead of on him. Sight removes the need for faith. We must write across our plans "if the Lord wills," and remember even good plans are poor substitutes for walking with Jesus.

Jim Rohn said we are the average of the five people we spend the most time with. Is Jesus one of your five? The more we include him in our thoughts, the more our desires reflect his (Ps. 37:4). Pursuing him changes our goals.

As Abraham followed God, his desire for God's promises intensified. He fretted when he couldn't see how the promise would be fulfilled (Gen. 15:2-3). God drew Abraham's eyes back on him, and Abraham's faith soared (Gen. 15:5-6).

God's call for us to leave California was well defined. But the second and third legs of our journey didn't become clear until it was time to take them. Many times, I've wanted God to reveal more of his plan ahead of time. But God wants me to focus on him. He supplies the grace I need when I need it.

God's call to Abraham reminds us to be more focused on our Guide than our goal. Jesus works out his plans for us when we keep in step with him (Ps. 138:8).

Scripture Reading...

Genesis 12:1–5

Acts 7:2–4

Study and Reflection

1. How would Abraham know when he reached the place God wanted him to go (Gen. 12:1)?

2. When our family visited Geneva, Switzerland, one-way streets and unintelligible signs kept us driving in circles, even though we knew our intended destination. What is the difference between having an address and having a trusted guide?

3. Judaism, Islam, and Christianity trace back to Abraham. Abraham's descendants blessed the world with the Law, the prophets, the Bible, and with Jesus. Because we know Abraham as a great name, it is easy to forget Abraham began with only a promise and a call. Name seven promises God gave Abraham (Gen. 12:2–3).

4. God's instructions to Abraham show he was not sending him off with a pat on the head and "Good luck." Notice the "I" phrases in Genesis 12:1–3 that refer to God. What is God's part in contrast to Abraham's? How does this apply to your life?

5. Abraham lived in Ur when God told him to leave (Acts 7:2–3). He traveled as far as Haran and settled there until his father, Terah, died. "Abram was seventy-five years old when he set

out from Harran" (Gen. 12:4). Abraham set off with God on a new adventure at an age when most people retire. As one of Abraham's children by faith, do you believe God wants to bless the world—even future generations—through you? Realizing that God accomplishes the result and our part is simply to go where he sends us, how does this change the way you see yourself and God's purpose for you?

6. Relate the Lord's promise in Matthew to Abraham and to us. "And everyone who has left houses or brothers or sisters or father or mother or wife or children or fields for my sake will receive a hundred times as much and will inherit eternal life" (Matt. 19:29).

What's Better than a GPS?
I could bake a cake in the time it takes to find the right hardware at a large local store. If I find a salesclerk, he'll point to a section of the store and leave me to figure out the rest. *Groan.*

At Whole Foods, an available worker stops stocking shelves and walks me to the item. It's much better to have an escort—even when you know what you're looking for.

God promised to show Abraham where to go. He didn't provide a map or a GPS so Abraham could calculate the time it would take or check his progress. Abraham had no idea what lay ahead. He didn't need to. His Friend had it covered. All he had to do was stick with his Friend.

When Larry's master's program was ending, he contacted the late Jim Craddock, founder of Scope Ministries. Jim invited us to join him in Amsterdam for Billy Graham's Amsterdam '86 conference. Spending time with Jim's staff during the conference confirmed that Scope was our next step. This took us to Oklahoma City for more training.

While in Oklahoma, an earlier pull to North Carolina resurfaced. We didn't know anyone there, but we both felt the tug. After Larry prayed over a North Carolina map, he met with Jim, who asked if he had thought about the exact area the Lord had laid on Larry's heart.

My Scope trainer introduced us to her friends in Raleigh. They invited us to spend a week with them and introduced us to their church home group. Several from the group said they had prayed for biblical counselors to come to the area. Was that the draw we'd felt? We put a deposit on a lot for a house the day before we returned to Oklahoma. God had shown us the next step.

When I walk with my Friend who knows the way, I'll get where I'm going at his appointed time. Sometimes, I have to remind myself to focus more on my Companion than on my timetable or the destination. Interruptions and detours may be part of his plan.

Faith journeys often include small beginnings with unknown endings. What would Abraham have missed if he'd stayed planted until God answered all of his questions? What will you and I miss if we delay obedience until sight replaces faith? Faith gave Abraham assurance of what he could not see. It will do the same for you and me.

CLOSING PRAYER

Use this space to turn your insights and responses into prayers.

I Want to Remember . . .

What do you want to remember from today's study?

Day Three
God's Friends Draw Close to God

Have you ever looked at a seasoned saint, marveled at her settled trust in the Lord, and wondered if you'll ever get there? Grass zips to maturity, but it takes decades to grow a mighty oak. Abraham reminds us that the progression to deep faith and friendship with God is a process, not instantaneous.

Abraham didn't model perfection, but he walked with God in the right direction. In spite of some awkward setbacks, Abraham's faith and friendship with God kept growing.

The development of Abraham's faith spanned decades. Bible commentator Kent Hughes says Abraham had lived in Canaan ten years when the Lord came to him with the promise that led to the moment he believed the Lord. "And the Lord counted him as righteous because of his faith" (Gen. 15:6 NLT).

It took another thirty years before the roots of his faith reached deep enough to support the offering of his son Isaac.

> Don't you remember that our ancestor Abraham was shown to be right with God by his actions when he offered his son Isaac on the altar? You see, his faith and his actions worked together. His actions made his faith complete. And so it happened just as the Scriptures say: "Abraham believed God, and God counted him as righteous because of his faith." He was even called the friend of God. (James 2:21–23 NLT)

God told Abraham to leave his family. For whatever reason, Abraham brought his nephew Lot with him. Lot's presence grieved Abraham on more than one occasion. (We'll learn more about that later.) Lot's immaturity was shocking. He preferred friendship with the world to closeness with God.

Do you want the faith of Abraham or Lot? Sustaining faith is rooted in our friendship with God. Friendship with the world weakens us.

Scripture Reading...

Hebrews 11:9
Genesis 12:6–9
Genesis 13:3–4

Study and Reflection

1. According to the following, what makes it possible for us to be friends with God? "For since our friendship with God was restored by the death of his Son while we were still his enemies, we will certainly be saved through the life of his Son. So now we can rejoice in our wonderful new relationship with God because our Lord Jesus Christ has made us friends of God" (Rom. 5:10–11 NLT).

2. What benefit do God's friends have over those who aren't close to him? "I no longer call you slaves, because a master doesn't confide in his slaves. Now you are my friends, since I have told you everything the Father told me" (John 15:15 NLT).

3. "A friend loves at all times" (Prov. 17:17). God warned, comforted, and guided Abraham throughout his life. How have you benefited from friendship with God?

4. Our faith walk with God includes layovers. What habit helped Abraham stay connected with God on every stop (Gen. 12:6–9)?

5. What safeguards help or could help you stay connected with Christ?

Jesus Calls Us Friend

Jesus calls you his friend. Isn't that staggering? Understanding how Jesus views us will change how we view ourselves and how we live.

If you want to develop mighty faith, focus on your friendship with Christ. Biblical faith and friendship with Jesus grow together. Practice his presence. Talk to him throughout the day. Ask him your questions. Establish a place to meet together. Seek his help and assurance. Abraham did. God wants that with you too.

The better we know him, the more we'll trust him. He takes our small steps of faith and creates in and through us something better than we can imagine.

CLOSING PRAYER

Use this space to turn your insights and responses into prayers.

I Want to Remember . . .

What do you want to remember from today's study?

Day Four

God's Friends Aren't Perfect

Sometimes we confuse a calling with instant maturity. God's calling doesn't remove the need for personal growth. What kind of expectations have you put on yourself or others who follow Christ? Abraham had to grow just like all of us—one step of faith at a time.

God commended Abraham's faith, but the Bible records some embarrassing blunders that came from his flesh. Have you ever made a bad decision because of fear? Me too. Fear distorts our thinking. It prompts actions that contradict our faith.

During a famine, instead of seeking God's counsel, Abraham sought relief in Egypt. He told Sarah to say she was his sister, so no one would kill him in order to take her. His deception brought wealth—and trouble. I wonder how Sarah felt when Abraham accepted sheep, cattle, and servants in exchange for her.

This happened twice! Both times, God swooped in with a miraculous intervention and rescued Sarah before these would-be bridegrooms consummated their marriages with her (Gen. 20:1–18). Both times, unbelieving rulers rebuked Abraham for deceiving them. Ouch. If godly Abraham made mistakes in protecting Sarah, maybe we should extend a little grace to our spouses—and to ourselves—when we make mistakes.

The strong undertow of the world and the flesh constantly pull us away from faith. We need to clutch the Lord's strong hand tighter when we feel threatened.

How do we live in the world and not be polluted by it? What do faith and wisdom look like when we face real challenges?

Abraham felt pressures similar to those we feel. Despite his stumbles, God commended him for living like a stranger in a foreign land. This strange acclamation will make more sense when we contrast him with his nephew Lot tomorrow.

Scripture Reading..
GENESIS 12:10–20; 13:1–4

Study and Reflection

1. What did Abraham predict would happen when they got into Egypt that caused him to ask Sarah to lie about their relationship?

2. What apparent good and bad results came from this lie?

3. Things seemed to play out just as Abraham had assumed. But how did this scheme jeopardize Sarah? What could have happened to her?

4. We aren't told whether Abraham and Sarah prayed for deliverance from this mess. How did God rescue them (Gen. 12:17)?

5. How were Abraham's assumptions about what the Egyptians would do proven wrong?

6. God chose Abraham to be a blessing to all nations; yet, when fear directed his choices, many suffered and he was humiliated in front of this king's court (Gen. 12:17–20). Christians represent Christ to the world. Do you remember a time when a believer's sin (maybe your own) hurt or harmed others? What warning do you take from this?

7. Abraham must have blushed in shame when a pagan ruler reprimanded him and kicked him out of Egypt. But he understood God's character (Ps. 103:3, 8–14). What did Abraham do to reconnect with God after he left Egypt (Gen. 13:1–4)?

8. God promised to give Abraham's descendants the land where he dwelt (Gen. 12:7). There is no record that Abram asked God for guidance when a famine came. Have your circumstances ever seemed to contradict God's promises? What does God promise in the following? "If you need wisdom, ask our generous God, and he will give it to you. He will not rebuke you for asking. But when you ask him, be sure that your faith is in God alone. Do not waver, for a person with divided loyalty is as unsettled as a wave of the sea that is blown and tossed by the wind" (James 1:5–6 NLT).

9. What personal applications do you take from this passage?

10. Has fear motivated you to take some actions you now regret? Ask God to rescue you and bring you back into the center of his will.

Our Faithful Friend

The Scripture promises, "If we are faithless, he remains faithful, for he cannot disown himself" (2 Tim. 2:13). God remained faithful to Abraham even when fear temporarily dimmed Abraham's faith.

The wealth Abraham gathered on his trip to Egypt created problems for him. Hagar was probably among the female servants Pharaoh gave Abraham. We'll discuss the trouble that came from Abraham's relationship with her next week. In addition, his many cattle and sheep created a turf war with his nephew Lot.

Perhaps Abraham learned to live as a stranger by some of his mistakes. Abraham's stumbles were part of his growth. As a friend said, "My breaking was my making."

I believe God recorded Abraham's missteps to remind us that Abraham was just like us. As God counted this imperfect man his friend, so Jesus calls his followers friends. Our inconsistencies can't break the special bond held together by our Savior's faithfulness.

CLOSING PRAYER

Use this space to turn your insights and responses into prayers.

I Want to Remember . . .

Today's takeaways from #LittleFaithBigGod are:

Day Five

God's Friends Aren't Home Here

"Aim at Heaven and you will get Earth 'thrown in';
aim at Earth and you will get neither."
—C. S. Lewis

God told Abraham to leave his country and family. Abraham left home, but took his father and nephew with him. Was that partial obedience, or does it show that leaving may be a process?

God didn't chastise Abraham for taking them, but he didn't show Abraham where to go until after Abraham's father died. Would he have arrived sooner if he'd left his father with his brother Nahor? We don't know. We do know God was going to get Abraham where he wanted him, and the process included forward and backward steps.

When God calls us into a relationship with him, he asks us to leave the country of unbelief. Sometimes Cousin Doubt and Sister Insecurity tag along. The closer we walk with Christ, the more these vestiges of our former life don't fit. Hanging onto them slows down our progress to spiritual maturity.

Abraham and Lot Split

Dr. James Dobson once said, "It takes a steady hand to hold a full cup." Possessions can possess us. How many families have parted over inheritance disputes? Like termites, a lust for stuff weakens our love for God.

While Abraham grew close to God, Lot buddied up with the world. He valued material ease and security over faith in God and a relationship with Uncle Abraham. He chose to raise his family in a prosperous, wicked city. His decision brought the devastating loss of his wife, home, possessions, and moral compass. He offered his virgin daughters to a mob to sexually abuse as they wished in order to protect his guests. No one respected him. His own family didn't listen when he tried to save them from destruction. His daughters got him drunk and slept with him to preserve their family line.

Randy Alcorn said, "When Jesus warns us not to store up treasures on earth, it's not just because wealth *might* be lost; it's because wealth will *always* be lost. Either it leaves us while we live, or we leave it when we die. No exceptions."[1] Lot surely illustrates this. In contrast, Abraham possessed worldly wealth, but his treasure was in heaven.

God is pleased to be called the God of Abraham. But we never refer to him as the God of Lot, even though the New Testament calls Lot righteous (2 Pet. 2:7).

Living as a stranger means refusing the world's values and ways. It means practicing God's methods even when they're unpopular and appear impractical. It may include setting boundaries in relationships—even with family members—as Abraham did with Lot (1 Cor. 15:33).

Comedian George Burns once quipped, "Happiness is having a large, loving, caring, close-knit family—in another city." Neighboring tribes witnessed the squabbles between Abraham's and Lot's herders (Gen. 13:5–18). Abraham suggested a peaceable parting to protect their relationship. Some relationships need distance. This is especially true when the parties embrace different values.

Abraham never stopped loving Lot. One time, he risked his men and his life to rescue his nephew when he learned four warring kings had kidnapped Lot. But he couldn't change Lot's heart and had to put distance between them.

Peter wrote, "Dear friends, I urge you, as foreigners and exiles, to abstain from sinful desires, which wage war against your soul" (1 Pet. 2:11). Abraham lived as an alien in this world because he was looking for heaven. Lot allowed the pleasures of this world to choke his faith.

Scripture Reading...
HEBREWS 11:9–10
GENESIS 13:5–18
JAMES 4:4

Study and Reflection

1. Contrast Abraham and Lot in Genesis 13:5–18.

2. What governed Lot's choice (Gen. 13:1–13)?

3. How does Abraham demonstrate faith in God in this squabble?

4. How did God reassure Abraham after this painful parting (Gen. 13:14–18)?

5. When God first called Abraham, he told him to leave his family (Gen. 12:1), but Abraham brought Lot with him. Lot's move to Sodom solved the squabbling but didn't end Abraham's problems with him. What lessons or applications do you draw from Abraham's dealings with Lot?

6. Abraham and Lot's different values and possessions caused friction. Do you have a relationship that would benefit from some space? Have possessions ever robbed you of happiness and good relationships?

The Prince Who Dwelt in Tents

Even in Abraham's day, most people lived in houses. Bible scholar Dr. Steve Anderson wrote, "If Abraham was a wealthy man in Ur, as he appears to have been, he must have possessed many treasures of the finest craftsmanship and the most exquisite materials. He would have lived in a mansion in Ur that would probably still look impressive today."[2] But Abraham patiently waited on God's timing to possess the land. His descendants didn't receive it until hundreds of years after Abraham's and the patriarchs' deaths. In fact, not until the end of the age when Jesus sets up his millennial kingdom will Abraham and his many descendants finally possess all the land God promised.

What a strange promise. The land is yours, but not in this lifetime. Abraham knew God was eternal and looked forward to living with him in heaven. Every day, his tents showed the world and reminded him that he wasn't home yet.

How Do We Live with a Tent Mind-Set?

Polyurethane fumes assaulted my nose when I opened my car door. After being out of town, I couldn't wait to see our refinished floors. Peeking through the windows, my stomach folded. The color was much lighter than I'd pictured. The vent grates drying on the front porch confirmed my fears. *How could this happen? He promised he'd match the color I'd shown him.*

I had to wait another twenty-four hours before I could go inside. I drove away feeling sick.

While I waited, Abraham's story spoke to me. "By faith . . . he lived in tents. . . . For he was looking forward to the city with foundations, whose architect and builder is God" (Heb. 11:9–10).

While living in tents, Abraham was looking for a city "with foundations." A tent has no foundations. No one expects the comforts of home while camping. Abraham didn't even try to make the promised land his home. He lived as a visitor.

There are benefits to viewing our homes and bodies as temporary tents until we get our real homes in heaven. In my few camping experiences, no one ever complained that a tent color clashed with a sleeping bag. Life's disappointments don't seem so big when we remember they're fleeting and the joy that awaits us is eternal.

While I waited to see my refinished floors, I asked the Lord to make me more like Abraham. I wanted joy in my journey and needed help to live like heaven was my real home. I counted my blessings and knew I wouldn't trade one of them for a different color floor.

Sunday, after church, the floors were dry enough to walk on. Two friends met me for moral support. The floors were beautiful. Lighter than I'd pictured—but they were the most beautiful tent floors I've ever seen!

We don't have to live in tents to have a tent mind-set. Remembering we aren't home yet carries us through the hassles of this life and helps us focus on what matters most.

CLOSING PRAYER

Use this space to turn your insights and responses into prayers.

I Want to Remember . . .

Today's takeaways from #LittleFaithBigGod are:

Prayer Requests

How to Know God Loves You

Stargazing

Count the stars? Impossible! But Abraham continued to gaze into the heavens anyway. The cold lump of disappointment he'd carried melted as he watched new stars emerge.

Belief warmed his core and spilled out in laughter and tears. Yes, he would become the father of many. The Creator, the One who spoke worlds into being, would do this.

MY TEENAGED HEART AWOKE TO GOD WHILE LYING ON MY back on a dock staring at stars visible only to someone away from city lights. The smell of the marsh, the rhythmic lap of the river, and the chirping night symphony cast a spell that made me feel small, yet part of something magnificent. David surely felt this magic when he wrote, "The heavens declare the glory of God; the skies proclaim the work of his hands" (Ps. 19:1).

Abraham also felt it. "For the Scriptures tell us, 'Abraham believed God, and God counted him as righteous because of his faith'" (Rom. 4:3 NLT). Genesis says this happened while he gazed at the stars.

Abraham had just defeated four wicked kings to rescue Lot, and he'd given up his rightful monetary reward. Perhaps he worried these kings would seek retribution. Or, in hindsight, had he been foolish not to take his fair share of the booty? Maybe he was just worn out from battle. Whatever his state, God understood and said, "Don't fear, Abraham. I am your great reward."

Now, if God spoke to you and said he was your great reward, how would you respond? Would you bow speechless and amazed? Would you leap for joy?

Abraham said, "Sovereign LORD, what can you give me since I remain childless?" (Gen. 15:2). In other words, "What I want is a son."

"What can you give me?" Whoa, Abraham. Don't you know to whom you're talking?

His reply reminds me of the little girl who prayed, "Thank you for the baby brother—but I prayed for a puppy."

Abraham wanted a son. Did his frankness offend God? No. Abraham and God were close. Abraham didn't need to fake a pious response. God understood his disappointments and longings. Dinah Maria Craik's poetic lines in *A Life for a Life* express the realness friendship with God provides:

> Oh, the comfort—the inexpressible comfort of feeling
> *safe* with a person—having neither to weigh thoughts
> nor measure words, but pouring them all right out,
> just as they are, chaff and grain together; certain that a
> faithful hand will take and sift them, keep what is worth
> keeping, and then with the breath of kindness blow the
> rest away.

This week, we continue our walk with Abraham and witness the continued growth of his faith.

Day One

God Fulfills Our Deepest Longings

God promised Abraham a son and said, "Now look toward the heavens, and count the stars, if you are able to count them."

I picture a long pause as Abraham considered the starry hosts. "And He said to him, 'So shall your descendants be.' Then he believed in the LORD; and He reckoned it to him as righteousness" (Gen. 15:5–6 NASB).

Why would counting billions of stars help Abraham believe he would father a son? God gave Isaiah similar instructions. "Look up into the heavens. Who created all the stars? He brings them out like an army, one after another, calling each by its name. Because of his great power and incomparable strength, not a single one is missing" (Isa. 30:26 NLT).

Notice the scene with Abraham again.

"Now look . . . and count the stars, if you are able to count them." Then Abraham "*believed in the Lord.*"

Abraham began to count the stars and was overcome. *Who was this who spoke to him?* Nothing was impossible to the Creator of all of this. The New American Standard Bible says he believed *in* God, and God counted his faith as righteousness.

The promise of a son was no longer remote when Abraham saw the size of God. The promise of great nations coming from an infertile couple was nothing to the Creator of the Milky Way.

In the end, God took Abraham's weakness and turned it into a staggering promise. Not one heir, Abraham—billions.

What has discouraged you or left you feeling powerless? Have you brought it to God? Maybe it's time for a little stargazing. Impossible problems are no problem for a big God.

Today we look at Abraham's faith and how it relates to righteousness.

Scripture Reading..
Genesis 15:1–6

Study and Reflection

1. The Bible reveals a righteousness that is available to those who will receive it. What did Abraham discover about being made right with God, and how does this apply to you personally? "Abraham was, humanly speaking, the founder of our Jewish nation. What did he discover about being made right with God? If his good deeds had made him acceptable to God, he would have had something to boast about. But that was not God's way. For the Scriptures tell us, 'Abraham believed God, and God counted him as righteous because of his faith.' When people work, their wages are not a gift, but something they have earned. But people are counted as righteous, not because of their work, but because of their faith in God who forgives sinners" (Rom. 4:1–5 NLT).

2. A wedding ring is a symbol of fidelity. But wearing one won't make a person faithful. In Paul's day, some insisted Gentile believers must be circumcised. Tomorrow, we'll look at Abraham's circumcision. From the following, what was the purpose of circumcision? "Circumcision was a sign that Abraham already had faith and that God had already accepted him and declared him to be righteous—even before he was circumcised. So Abraham is the spiritual father of those who have faith but have not been circumcised. They are counted as righteous because of their faith. And Abraham is also the spiritual father of those who have been

circumcised, but only if they have the same kind of faith Abraham had before he was circumcised" (Rom. 4:11–12 NLT).

3. Some religious people in Paul's day substituted symbols of faith for a relationship with Christ. Ask the Lord to show you if you have done that in an area and how to return to simple faith.

4. How was God able to make Abraham the father of many nations? "That is what the Scriptures mean when God told him, 'I have made you the father of many nations.' This happened because Abraham believed in the God who brings the dead back to life and who creates new things out of nothing. Even when there was no reason for hope, Abraham kept hoping—believing that he would become the father of many nations. For God had said to him, 'That's how many descendants you will have!'" (Rom. 4:17–18 NLT).

5. Notice Abraham's remarkable faith. "And Abraham's faith did not weaken, even though, at about 100 years of age, he figured his body was as good as dead—and so was Sarah's womb. Abraham never wavered in believing God's promise. In fact, his faith grew stronger, and in this he brought glory to God. He was fully convinced that God is able to do whatever he promises" (Rom. 4:19–21 NLT). If Abraham's faith was based on what he saw, it would have weakened as he and Sarah aged. Is there an issue that has gone from bad to

worse since you began praying over it? How can you apply Abraham's faith to your challenge?

6. Even though Abraham's actions sometimes missed the mark, God counted him as righteous because of his faith. How does Abraham's faith relate to how we become righteous? "And because of Abraham's faith, God counted him as righteous. And when God counted him as righteous, it wasn't just for Abraham's benefit. It was recorded for our benefit, too, assuring us that God will also count us as righteous if we believe in him, the one who raised Jesus our Lord from the dead. He was handed over to die because of our sins, and he was raised to life to make us right with God" (Rom. 4:22–25 NLT).

The Strength of Weakness

Not being able to get what we want with our own strength carries benefits. Abraham and Sarah couldn't produce a son the natural way. They had to rely on God. Faith, not sight, kept their hope alive.

Which is the greater challenge for God: To create a child from a couple past childbearing ages or to change a sinner into a saint? To heal a broken bone or to heal a broken heart? Nothing is "too hard for the LORD" (Gen. 18:14). It doesn't matter if your challenge is physical, spiritual, or relational; the God of Abraham has the power to create something new.

As Abraham's faith enabled him to have a son at age one hundred, our faith empowers us to "produce love, joy, peace, patience, kindness, goodness, faithfulness, gentleness, and self-control" (Gal. 5:22–23 NLT) and to make disciples through the Holy Spirit's power (Acts 1:8). Faith keeps hope vibrant when circumstances appear hopeless.

Abraham's faith grew stronger as his situation grew bleaker. It is as though he said, "Wow, God, this is going to be some miracle." And it was.

Our inability to gain what we want can discourage us or refocus us. If something I want is not God's will, then do I really want it? If it is his will, then can my helplessness stop God's power? Instead of asking, "Am I able?" we ask, "Am I available?" Focusing on being *available* instead of on being *able* plants my trust in his ability, not my own.

Have you been standing on a promise and things now look worse instead of better? Remember Abraham and let your impossible situation feed your faith. Life-giving power is released through faith.

CLOSING PRAYER

Lord Jesus, thank you that your power is not limited by time, circumstances, or my lack. Use this space to turn your insights and responses into prayers.

I Want to Remember . . .

Today's takeaways from #LittleFaithBigGod are:

Day Two

God Redeems Our Stumbles

Sarah means "princess."

"God said you would have a son. Did he say I would have a son?" Sarah asked.

Abraham closed his eyes and massaged his temples. Finally, he shook his head. "No, he didn't name you."

"See," Sarah pressed. "We know it's God's will for you to have a son. I'm barren. Abram, please, be sensible. Take Hagar." Sarah reached for Abram's hands, freckled with age. "We'll have a family. Isn't that what God wants? How many more years can we afford to wait?"

Have you ever tried to help God? Maybe you wanted to help a friend know Christ or help your child come out of her shell. Noble goals—but your scheming backfired. If so, you can relate to Abraham and Sarah.

Many years passed after God promised Abraham a son and still there was no child. His other promises rested on this child. How could the world be blessed through his descendants if he had none? They waited and waited and still nothing. Sarah remained barren.

I can imagine Sarah and Abraham's conversation. Temptations appear so reasonable in the moment. Having children through a wife's maidservant was common practice in that culture. They would be one big happy family—or so they thought.

Abraham was a man of faith. But in the incident with Hagar, the object of his faith slipped. He tried to accomplish God's promise without God. He thought he could produce spiritual fruit through human effort. Instead, he brought ongoing grief to many.

One Big Mess

Sarah had used Hagar to get a baby for herself. Hagar despised Sarah when she realized she wouldn't even be elevated to the status of a wife. Sarah lashed back at her maidservant with harsh treatment. Instead of the harmony they had imagined, hostility reigned.

Jesus said, "Human effort accomplishes nothing" (John 6:63 NLT). Abraham eventually had to send away the son born from their scheming.

I empathize with Sarah and Abraham. Whenever God's revealed will doesn't match my timetable, I want to speed things along. I'm still learning the difference between persevering and striving. When does faith push through obstacles, and when does it patiently wait on God?

I've learned to check my inner motivations. Faith is not desperate. It doesn't rush God in order to relieve my doubts (Isa. 5:18–19). It responds quickly to God's promptings, yet "whoever believes will not be in haste" (Isa. 28:16 ESV).

One of the best ways to discern his will is to ask him if a nudge is from him and then open our Bibles. God's leading won't violate his principles, and faith doesn't scheme or manipulate.

Jesus told those who wanted to do the works of God, "This is the only work God wants from you: Believe in the one he has sent" (John 6:29 NLT). God doesn't need my help; he wants my faith.

When we feel pressured to act, the following considerations can protect us:

- Ask the Holy Spirit if the prompting you feel is Spirit-led or flesh-driven.
- The flesh drives us with thoughts such as *It's up to me* and produces the fear of missing out, urgency, and desperation.

- Faith reminds me God will accomplish what concerns me (Ps. 138:8) and produces love, joy, peace, patience, kindness, goodness, faithfulness, gentleness, and self-control (Gal. 5:22–23).

God Works All Things Together for the Good

God never chastened or condemned Abraham for this episode, but neither did he step in and stop the natural consequences. The conflict in the Middle East between the descendants of Issac and Ishmael is an ongoing result of Abraham and Sarah's actions. Abraham felt the painful fallout of his fleshly choice. It hurt when he had to send Hagar and Ishmael away. He'd already had to separate from his nephew Lot. But God didn't waste this mistake. He used it to illustrate spiritual truths (Gal. 4:24–26, 30–31).

Human strivings never produce fruit, only painful thorns that draw blood. But God works even those thorns together for the good of those who love him (Rom. 8:28). Since he did it for Abraham, we can trust him to work our foolish mistakes together for our good too.[1]

Scripture Reading..

Hebrews 11:11–12
Genesis 17:1–27; 21:1–21

Study and Reflection

1. God changed Abram's and Sarai's names. Abram means "exalted father." Abraham means "father of many." What new part of his plan did God reveal to ninety-nine-year-old Abraham (Gen. 17:15–16, 19)?

2. How did Abraham respond to this news (Gen. 17:17–18)?

3. What did God promise concerning Ishmael (Gen. 17:20)?

4. How did Abraham exhibit his faith in God (Gen. 17:10–11, 23–27)?

5. When did the promised son finally arrive (Gen. 21:2)? What do you take from that?

6. Sarah saw Ishmael mocking Isaac and demanded Abraham send him away. (Ishmael would have been fifteen or sixteen by this time.) This upset Abraham very much (Gen. 21:8–14). How do Abraham's actions show his growing faith and hope in the future?

7. Ishmael was the product of human effort. He was not the son God had promised. Yet he was Abraham's son. How does God show mercy to Abraham, Hagar, and Ishmael (Gen. 21:15–21)?

8. How was sending Ishmael away an act of faith?

Sending Ishmael Away

My stomach tightened. Within an hour, two unconnected people had frowned over my ideas on different topics. Their questions didn't make me doubt my views, but their implied disapproval felt bad. The story of Abraham and Ishmael spoke to me.

It distressed Abraham to send Ishmael away. He'd already parted with Lot, who had, no doubt, been like a son to him. Abraham wanted God to fulfill his promises through Ishmael.

The Apostle Paul wrote that Ishmael represents the fruitless deeds of human effort, and Isaac represents those born according to the Spirit. After Isaac's birth, Abraham had to send Ishmael away because the flesh and the Spirit oppose each other. "Ishmael, the child born by human effort, persecuted Isaac, the child born by the power of the Spirit" (Gal. 4:29 NLT).

But it hurt to send Ishmael away.

What does Ishmael have to do with us? Ishmael represents our human effort to make life work. Human striving produces Ishmaels, not Isaacs. Pleasing people is my Ishmael. It's uncomfortable to let go of what I've relied upon.

Paul wrote, "Am I now trying to win the approval of human beings, or of God? Or am I trying to please people? If I were still trying to please people, I would not be a servant of Christ" (Gal. 1:10). The little word "still" shows that Paul once tried to please people, but he was able to replace that with seeking to please God. My reaction told me that even though I wanted to please God, I cared too much about what others thought.

My friend, whom I'll call Kaylee, had a different Ishmael. Her estranged father was her Ishmael. After he abandoned the family, her mother kept him away. Kaylee grieved the loss of her daddy. Years later, she realized that painful separation had protected her from his abusive, alcoholic behavior.

Whether our Ishmael is a destructive pattern or a person, it hurts to release something or someone we care about—even when it's harmful. But we must let go. God told Abraham not to be distressed over the boy—he would take care of him and make him into a great nation (Gen. 17:20).

In adulthood, Kaylee reached out to her dad and saw him trust Christ shortly before his death. She knows they have eternity to make up for what they missed on earth.

In order to walk with the Lord, Abraham had to leave his home and family. Later, to stay in step with God, he had to send his son Ishmael away. (Tomorrow we'll see why Isaac had to be Abraham's only child.) We must send away our Ishmaels in order to experience God's best too. The pain of losing Ishmael can't compare to the agony of keeping him. "No discipline seems pleasant at the time, but painful. Later on, however, it produces a harvest of righteousness and peace for those who have been trained by it" (Heb. 12:11).

CLOSING PRAYER

Use this space to turn your insights and responses into prayers.

I Want to Remember . . .

Today's takeaways from #LittleFaithBigGod are:

Day Three
God Asks Us to Trust Him

*"It was by faith that Abraham offered Isaac as
a sacrifice when God was testing him."*
—Hebrews 11:17 (NLT)

Dressed in blue Superman pajamas complete with a red cape, our three-year-old, Brant, thought he could fly. He leaped off furniture onto my cousin's and his friend's backs. One day, Brant fell off of a tall slide and bumped his head. Because he couldn't remember what happened, I told him we needed to go to the emergency room. He flailed, argued, and refused to cooperate.

"It will be all right. We have to go," I said, puzzled at his resistance. He quieted and climbed into the car.

The door swooshed shut with the doctor's exit. Brant turned his brown eyes to me. "Is he going to cut off my legs now?"

"You hurt your head," I said. "Why would he cut off your legs?"

"Oh. Is he going to cut off my head?"

My breath caught. Our neighbor's legs had been amputated at a hospital. Brant associated hospitals with amputation. No wonder he'd panicked when I said he had to go to the hospital.

I swallowed the lump of emotion lodged in my throat. My son had trusted me even when he believed he'd lose his legs.

Abraham, one of the greatest heroes of the faith, practiced childlike faith. He trusted his Father, even when asked to offer up his only son. "So anyone who becomes as humble as this little child is the greatest in the Kingdom of Heaven" (Matt. 18:4 NLT).

After waiting twenty-five long years to hold this baby, after memorizing every facial expression and savoring every giggle and antic, Abraham could have reasoned with God and begged for a different test. "How can you fulfill your promise if you take Isaac?

You've already sent Ishmael away. Take me, but, please, don't take our laughter away."

But Abraham didn't argue or bargain. He humbly trusted his heavenly Father. God had promised to give him descendants through Isaac. And God would keep his promise. Abraham's child-like faith was stronger than a mighty oak.

Scripture Reading...

HEBREWS 11:17–19
GENESIS 22:1–19

Study and Reflection

1. While the devil's temptations often make perfect sense at the time, God's tests defy reason. How did God's instructions to offer Isaac as a burnt offering seem to counter his previous promises to Abraham (Heb. 11:17–19)?

2. Record your observations and thoughts on Genesis 22:1–19.

3. What does Abraham's response to God's request reveal about him (Gen. 22:3)?

Is God Ever Cruel?

When my Bible study discussed this scene, several called it a cruel test. Since God is never sadistic, let's consider why God tested Abraham and why he tests us:

- To protect and purify our hearts. Even before God gave the Ten Commandments, Abraham intrinsically knew he could have no others gods before the Lord. As Jesus said, "No one can serve two masters. Either you will hate the one and love the other, or you will be devoted to the one and despise the other" (Matt. 6:24). Anyone or anything we love more than God harms us and diminishes our potential. God's test protected Abraham. "Don't transfer your hope onto Isaac."

- To testify to a watching world. Three major faiths trace back to Abraham. This story points to Jesus in a most affecting way and testifies to Abraham's belief in God's power to raise the dead. Trust in God provides hope and courage in the midst of pain and confusion, which attracts people's attention. How we face our trials may be our greatest witness to the world and to our loved ones.

- To reveal how much God loves Jesus—and us. Abraham offering his beloved son humanizes the story of God offering his only Son. A cruel test? God stopped Abraham from sacrificing Isaac, but he watched Jesus die on the cross. Fellowshipping with Jesus in our sufferings is one way we get to know him (Phil. 3:7–11). Tests draw us closer to God.

- To display the genuineness of our faith (1 Pet. 1:7). God wasn't trying to break Abraham. He was showcasing Abraham's faith. Tests show the genuineness our faith.

- To show the worthiness of Jesus. Abraham's worship showed he recognized Christ's worth. Faithfulness through pain shows that Jesus is worthy of our suffering.

Warren Wiersbe wrote, "Our greatest battles are not waged between love and hatred, but between two loves: our love for God and our love for God's blessings. And the deeper we love, the more difficult is the test."[2]

Childlike faith knows that God's tests are not punishments. "For you know that when your faith is tested, your endurance has a chance to grow. So let it grow, for when your endurance is fully developed, you will be perfect and complete, needing nothing" (James 1:3–4 NLT).

Abraham began his journey of faith by leaving his home, his family's gods, and his relatives in order to obey God. Through the decades, each act of obedience strengthened Abraham's trust in God. He circumcised his men. He lived as a stranger. He sent Ishmael away. Each test stretched Abraham the way exercise leaves you sore but stronger.

Abraham's grownup faith trusted his Father in the most childlike way. He packed his donkey and set off to sacrifice what he loved most in the world—because he loved God more than anything on earth. Do you love God more than his gifts? Do you trust him with what is most dear to you? Grown-up faith reveals itself in childlike trust.

CLOSING PRAYER

Use this space to turn your insights and responses into prayers.

I Want to Remember . . .

Today's takeaways from #LittleFaithBigGod are:

Day Four

God Loves Us Sacrificially

"Father, we're here," Isaac said. Abraham had never looked so weary. Was his father ill? His quietness during these three days of travel concerned Isaac.

Abraham nodded, wiped his crinkled eyes, and turned to his servants. "Stay here with the donkey while the boy and I go and worship. . . . " He dropped his head, then looked them in the eyes. "Then we will come back to you."

How could anyone ever doubt Abraham's love for God after he offered up his only son to him? Here's a more pertinent question: How can we ever doubt God's love for us when he offered up his only son for us?

When God described Isaac to Abraham, I hear him describing Jesus. This story, like no other, gives us a glimpse into what it cost the father heart of God to sacrifice his only Son for us.

Scripture Reading..
GENESIS 22:1–19

Study and Reflection

1. How did God describe Isaac in Genesis 22:2?

2. How is God's description of Isaac similar to his description of Jesus? "And a voice from heaven said, 'This is my dearly loved Son, who brings me great joy'" (Matt. 3:17 NLT).

3. How many days did Abraham carry the pending death of Isaac in his heart (Gen. 22:4)?

4. Do you see a connection between worship and sacrifice (Gen. 22:5)? What must you sacrifice in order to offer thanksgiving, praise, or service?

5. Isaac was a teenager, and Abraham was well past one hundred years old. Isaac, no doubt, could have outrun or overpowered his father. What does Genesis 22:9–10 say about Isaac?

6. What do you learn about God from Genesis 22:11–19?

Notable Parallels between the Sacrifice of Isaac and the Sacrifice of Jesus

This story of sacrifice parallels Jesus in many ways—only for Jesus, there was no ram in the thicket to take his place. He is the Lamb of God. As you read some of the parallels, don't miss the emotions these fathers and sons must have felt.

Jesus said, "Your father Abraham rejoiced to see My day, and he saw it and was glad" (John 8:56 NASB). I wonder if it was this event where Abraham saw Jesus.

Both Were Dearly Loved Only Sons

Isaac: "Take your son, your only son—yes, Isaac, whom you love so much—and go to the land of Moriah. Go and sacrifice him as a burnt offering" (Gen. 22:2 NLT).

Jesus: "And a voice from heaven said, 'This is my dearly loved Son, who brings me great joy'" (Matt. 3:17 NLT).

Third-Day Hope
Isaac: "On the third day Abraham looked up and saw the place in the distance. He said to his servants, 'Stay here . . . . We will come back to you'" (Gen. 22:4–5).

Jesus: "He must be killed and on the third day be raised to life" (Matt. 16:21).

Wood for the Sacrifice
Isaac: "Abraham took the wood for the burnt offering and placed it on his son Isaac" (Gen. 22:6).

Jesus: "Carrying his own cross, he went out to the place of the Skull" (John 19:17).

Father and Son Working Together
Isaac: "As the two of them went on together" (Gen. 22:6).

Jesus: "For God was in Christ, reconciling the world to himself" (2 Cor. 5:19 NLT).

Where Is the Lamb?
Isaac: "Isaac spoke up and said to his father Abraham, 'Father? . . . The fire and wood are here . . . but where is the lamb for the burnt offering?'" (Gen. 22:7).

Jesus: "'Abba, Father,' he cried out, 'everything is possible for you. Please take this cup of suffering away from me. Yet I want your will to be done, not mine'" (Mark 14:36 NLT).

God Would Provide the Lamb
Isaac: "Abraham answered, 'God himself will provide the lamb.' . . . Abraham looked up and there in a thicket he saw a ram caught by its horns" (Gen. 22:8, 13).

Jesus: "The next day John saw Jesus coming toward him and said, 'Look, the Lamb of God, who takes away the sin of the world!'" (John 1:29).

The Thorns
Isaac: The ram's head was caught in a thicket of thorns (Gen. 22:13).

Jesus: Jesus wore a crown of thorns (Matt. 27:29).

The Lord Will Provide
Isaac: The ram was sacrificed on Mount Moriah instead of Isaac (Gen. 22:2, 9). "So Abraham called that place The LORD Will Provide. And to this day it is said, 'On the mountain of the LORD it will be provided'" (Gen. 22:14).

Jesus: God provided his Son. "But now, once for all time, he [Christ] has appeared at the end of the age to remove sin by his own death as a sacrifice" (Heb. 9:26 NLT).

He Loves You Intensely
After reading this story, no one can doubt Abraham's devotion to God. When you question God's care for you, remember

- As Abraham so loved God that he gave his only son, God so loved you that he gave his only Son (John 3:16).
- As Isaac trusted his father and climbed onto the altar, so Jesus trusted his Father and stayed on the cross (John 10:17–18).

If we can't doubt Abraham's devotion to God, then how can we question our heavenly Father's love for us? Jesus knew there would be times we'd ask, "Lord, how much do you love me?" So he stretched out his arms on the cross and answered, "This much!"

CLOSING PRAYER

Has something caused you to question God's love for you? Bring that to him now. Choose to believe he will work your losses and mistakes together for your good and his glory. Receive his love.

I Want to Remember . . .

Today's takeaways from #LittleFaithBigGod are:

Day Five

God Finishes What He Begins

I never felt more helpless than when our babies' fevers spiked. Later, as teens, when they started driving, I prayed for their safety. Parents who watch their children go off to war have my deepest respect. Understanding the compulsion to protect our children makes Abraham's willingness to sacrifice Isaac all the more astounding.

Most parents who lose a child aren't given a choice. Abraham was asked to sacrifice his healthy son. Abraham had prayed and waited and waited for God to give him a son. Isaac arrived when Abraham was one hundred years old. Imagine the joy this miracle child brought Sarah and Abraham. The fulfillment of God's promises to Abraham lay in Isaac. Then God asked Abraham to do the inconceivable—sacrifice his one and only son.

By faith, Abraham obeyed.

He reasoned that *if* Isaac died, *God was able to bring him back to life again.* Abraham didn't have blind faith. He had logical faith. God would keep his promise. Abraham's descendants would come through Isaac. God would either rescue Isaac or raise him from the dead. Since God had the power to resurrect a dead womb, then God could resurrect a dead body. When he surrendered Isaac, he believed he'd see him again. He knew God would keep his promise.

Scripture Reading...
HEBREWS 11:17–19

Study and Reflection

1. Notice the plural subject in Abraham's declaration in Genesis. "We will worship and then we will come back to you." According to Hebrews 11:19, why was Abraham able to make such a declaration?

2. Paul wrote, "And I am certain that God, who began the good work within you, will continue his work until it is finally finished on the day when Christ Jesus returns" (Phil. 1:7 NLT). Remembering Abraham's journey of faith, how did God's work in Abraham from the time God first called him until the time he offered Isaac encourage you?

3. We've whizzed through some of the highs and lows of Abraham's life. How did his life encourage your faith?

4. What did you learn about friendship with God from Abraham?

Father Abraham

We've only touched on Abraham's life. For the most part, Abraham lived in the world but not as the world.

As someone in the world, he rescued kidnapped Lot. He interceded on behalf of Sodom. He acquired great assets. As one not of this world, he refused his rightful booty from the wicked king of Sodom and accepted only what his men earned. He gave a tenth to the priest of Salem. He trusted God to protect and provide for him. He believed God would keep his promises. The result was that, unlike Lot, his neighbors respected him (Gen. 23:6). What's more, God forever linked his name with Abraham.

Abraham's walk with God was not perfect. But it was genuine. After decades of walking with God, God knew Abraham was ready to display perfect faith.

God tests us like an engineer runs tests to prove his bridge will support the traffic it will receive. He tests us not to break us but to show what he has built.

Abraham's faith reminds us:

- God's ways are always best.
- We need an eternal perspective to appreciate God's ways.

Abraham was God's friend, and Jesus is our friend and a brother. "Greater love has no one than this: to lay down one's life for one's friend" (John 15:13). Next week, we will look more deeply into the hope our faith brings when we face death.

CLOSING PRAYER

Use this space to turn your insights and responses into prayers.

I Want to Remember . . .

Today's takeaways from #LittleFaithBigGod are:

Prayer Requests

How the Lost Boys Found Forever-Land

Abraham, Isaac, Jacob, and Joseph—Longing for Heaven

"Tomorrow is Mother's Day," Daddy said. "You might want to skip church." He turned away to wipe another tear from his cheek.

We'd laid Mama to rest that afternoon, under a lovely moss-draped oak that overlooked a peaceful waterway. Flowers and comfort food from caring friends still filled our home. It was the first quiet we'd had since she passed. Yet these external consolations failed to touch the ache that losing my mother to cancer and my father to grief had carved.

EVEN THOUGH I WAS STILL IN HIGH SCHOOL, I FELT RESPON-sible to step up and fill Mama's shoes after she died. I grocery shopped on the weekend. I wanted to alleviate Daddy's suffering.

Being responsible helped me not think about my loss by day. But my grief leaked out on my pillow at night, sometimes in my sleep.

Our family lived under the unwritten rule that light emotions were acceptable. We hid our grief and coped on our own. I think this aversion to expressing emotions played into my parents' not talking about the prognosis of my mother's illness. But dodging the topic of death didn't make it go away.

Hebrews 11 shows us we don't need to fear or avoid this subject. The patriarchs model how to die and how to prepare our loved ones for our death.

Day One
Dream-Shaking Death

Mammy's dining table held a Southern feast of fried chicken, butter beans, sliced tomatoes, homemade biscuits with melted butter, and sweet tea. Saucers of vanilla ice cream rounded off the meal. My family drove an hour after church to my maternal grandmother's house for Sunday dinner. Even though I didn't linger around the table, the memory of my family's laughter still warms me.

After Mammy died, Mama carried on the tradition of connecting around Mammy's table, often with aunts, uncles, and cousins. After Mama died, Daddy remarried. He cleaned out the house and gave away our furniture. A friend's family stored Mammy's table in their attic for me.

When I married, we U-Hauled the table across the country to our small apartment. Living on the other side of the country from my family, I imagined a day when my sister and I would gather with our own families and Daddy's belly laugh would delight us.

When Daddy died, my thoughts raced to my longing for family gatherings around Mammy's table. The picture had been so real; I couldn't believe it would never happen. Even at the time, those thoughts surprised me.

Maybe since death is too big to grasp, grief attaches to unexpected objects. A grieving mother who'd found a half-read book among her deceased son's belongings told me it haunted her that her son would never know how the book ended. A human life should not end before a book is finished. When the pansies Mama planted continued to bloom months after she was gone, I didn't know whether to love or hate them.

We were made for eternity, and death just doesn't sit well. If the grieving mother learned her son had finished the book, she would still grieve. If Mama had died after the pansies had faded, something else would have scraped my loss. I wish Daddy could have lived until all his grandchildren were born and we could have shared a meal as one big family, but he didn't. We are never ready to say good-bye to someone we love.

Memories associated with someone's passing etch themselves onto our souls. How someone faces death can communicate as much about them as how they lived. Biblical faith is practical not only for this life; it carries us into the next life. And it comforts those left behind. Let's look at how our view of God impacts how we face death and why how we die matters to our families after we're gone.

Scripture Reading..

HEBREWS 11:13–22

Study and Reflection

1. In what ways did the patriarchs see God as bigger than death?

2. How did their faith in God affect their experience in facing death (Heb. 11:1)?

3. Abraham's son and grandson, who inherited the promise, followed his example on how to live on earth and face death. Would you be happy if your children, grandchildren, and friends imitated your walk with God? What are some ways we can pass our faith on to our descendants? Walk *the walk;*

4. The patriarchs were foreigners and nomads here on earth, "longing for a better country—a heavenly one."

   a. Why does seeing ourselves as foreigners on earth change how we face death (Heb. 11:13–16)?

   b. Why do you think the patriarchs' longing for a heavenly country pleased God (Heb. 11:6, 16)? *✳*

5. To prepare means "to get everything ready." We prepare our homes and favorite foods for our families and friends to visit. We prepare ourselves for special gatherings.

   a. In regard to your own passing or someone else's, what does it mean to you to know God has prepared an eternal city for us? *My hope to see god + family again. meet Jesus.*

   b. How did the patriarchs prepare themselves for the gathering in heaven? *Lived by Faith.*

6. God knows us better than we know ourselves. From the following, do you think you will like what he has prepared for you? Why or why not?

   a. "That is what the Scriptures mean when they say, 'No eye has seen, no ear has heard, and no mind has imagined what God has prepared for those who love him'" (1 Cor. 2:9 NLT).

   b. "Do not let your hearts be troubled. You believe in God; believe also in me. My Father's house has many rooms; if that were not so, would I have told you that I am going there to prepare a place for you? And if I go and prepare a place for you, I will come back and take you to be with me that you also may be where I am" (John 14:1–3).

Hope in Grief

A teacher asked her second graders to write out prayers to God. One little girl wrote, "Instead of letting people die and having to make new ones, why don't you just keep the ones you have now?"

An older woman had a different take on death. When she met with her pastor to plan her funeral, she told him she wanted to be buried with a fork in her hand.

"A fork?"

"Yes," she said. "At church suppers when they collect the plates after dinner, if there's dessert they tell us to keep our forks. My fork says the best is yet to come."

Abraham, Isaac, Jacob, and Joseph shared the second view. Death for a believer isn't passing away; it's *passing on* to a better place.

We grieve when we lose a loved one. But Christians grieve with hope. Like the patriarchs, we believe in a resurrection and reunion. We know the experience of our loved one in heaven is better than any dream envisioned on earth (1 Cor. 2:9). Biblical faith changes how we live, die, and say good-bye. Pass the dessert, please!

CLOSING PRAYER

Use this space to turn your insights and responses into prayers.

I Want to Remember . . .

What do you want to remember from today's study? Let's encourage each other by sharing our takeaways on social media with the hashtag #LittleFaithBigGod.

Day Two

Isaac: Passing on the Blessing

Isaac means "to laugh."

Jacob entered Isaac's tent. Would his brother's clothing be enough to fool his blind father?

"How were you able to prepare the feast so quickly?" Isaac asked.

"The Lord your God gave me success," Jacob lied, glad his father couldn't see his burning cheeks. It didn't bother him to bolster his lie with God's name. He'd never claimed his father's God as his God. But he didn't want to be caught lying.

"Come close, my son. Let me touch you. Are you really Esau, my firstborn?" Isaac asked.

Jacob's breath caught. Would the goat hair on his hands pass for Esau's hands? Steady, he told himself. He's just being cautious.

If I were going to highlight Isaac's faith, I'd point out how he climbed onto the altar for Abraham. To submit to having your throat cut and body burned ranks high in bravery and faith in my book. I wouldn't have showcased him blessing Jacob. Isaac thought he was blessing Esau the first time he blessed Jacob!

Isaac knew which son God had chosen to receive the blessing given to Abraham. During his wife's pregnancy, Rebekah had asked the Lord about the wrestling she felt inside her womb. The Lord explained, "The sons in your womb will become two nations. From the very beginning, the two nations will be rivals. One nation will be stronger than the other; and your older son will serve your younger son" (Gen. 25:23 NLT).

Talk about a rascal—Isaac didn't agree with God's choice and plotted to go behind Rebekah's and God's backs. Even though Esau had "despised his birthright" (Gen. 25:34; Heb. 12:16–17), Isaac may have reasoned, *If God really wanted Jacob to inherit the blessing, he would have told me directly, not just Rebekah.* Isaac enjoyed eating wild game, and Esau was a hunter. Since Esau was born first, it seemed fair to give him the firstborn's double blessing. Whatever his excuse, Isaac conspired to bless his favorite son.

Isaac wasn't the only scamp in this family. Rebekah overheard her husband's plot and devised her own. She prepared a feast Isaac would love and told Jacob—her favorite son—to dress in Esau's clothes to serve it. I guess she forgot about Sarah and Abraham's grief with Hagar and Ishmael. She thought she could accomplish God's will by human strategies.

Before we look at how God overrode these schemers and resurrected Isaac's faith, let's return to the scene we started above.

Isaac patted his stomach and sighed, signaling his satisfaction with the meal. "How about a kiss from my number one son?" Isaac asked, pointing to his cheek.

Jacob leaned over and kissed his father. "Ah, the smell of my son is like the smell of the outdoors that the Lord has blessed!" Then Isaac blessed Jacob with all he longed to give Esau.

With ears alert for Esau's return, Jacob hardly heard the blessing he'd maneuvered to gain. It was a hollow victory, as he knew his father was thinking of Esau. What would happen when his father found out he'd tricked him?

Scripture Reading...

HEBREWS 11:20

GENESIS 25:21–28; 27:1–28:5; 28:10–15

Study and Reflection

1. God chose Jacob to father the stronger nation before the twins were born (Gen. 25:21–26). How does God's choosing of Jacob relate to his choosing of us? "When he [Isaac] married Rebekah, she gave birth to twins. But before they were born, before they had done anything good or bad, she received a message from God. (This message shows that God chooses people according to his own purposes; he calls people, but not according to their good or bad works.) She was told, 'Your older son will serve your younger son'" (Rom. 9:10–12 NLT). "Even before he made the world, God loved

us and chose us in Christ to be holy and without fault in his eyes" (Eph. 1:4 NLT). *God's will for me is not always the easy or the worldly or obvious*

2. What governed Isaac's pick (Gen. 25:27–28)? *his stomach!*

3. The flesh, not faith, fueled Isaac's effort to pass on the blessing to Esau (Gen. 25:21–26; 27:1–4). How did Isaac demonstrate genuine faith after he discovered Jacob's deception (Gen. 27:30–40; 28:1–5)? *accepted it.*

4. Apply Isaac to your life. Are you surprised God commended him for his faith in blessing Jacob? Or does his initial failing make his recovery more notable?

5. When Jacob fled Esau's wrath, God spoke to him in a dream and passed the blessing to him. From Genesis 28:10–15, explain why Jacob didn't need to deceive his father to receive the blessing.

6. God remained faithful to Jacob, even when Jacob was scheming and bargaining with him. But the Bible says we reap what we sow. Jacob fled from Esau (Gen. 27:41–45), and never saw his mother again. Jacob, who had deceived his father by pretending to be his older brother, in an ironic twist was tricked by his uncle on his wedding night. Instead of marrying the younger sister, who'd captured his love, Jacob woke up beside

her older sister. What do you learn from this family's faith and flaws?

7. Is there a situation in your life where, like Isaac, you think your choice is better than what God has chosen for you? How can you demonstrate faith in areas where your views clash with his?

[handwritten notes: pray to reveal God's will — w/ Daly — w/ Neighborhood — Pray, pray, pray & listen.]

Passing on the Blessing

Imagine Isaac's shock when, only moments after he'd finished blessing Jacob, Esau, eager to receive his father's blessing, triumphantly strode into his tent carrying the meal he'd prepared. How would you expect Isaac to respond when he realized his younger son had deceived him? Instead of exploding in anger, he roused in faith. He bowed his proud heart and accepted God's choice.

"I blessed Jacob—and, indeed, he will be blessed!" The angels cheered, and God applauded and exalted Isaac as an example of faith.

Isaac's words to his beloved Esau showed Isaac had accepted God's will: the nation that would come from Jacob would be greater than the one that would come from Esau. Before sending Jacob off to find a wife, he blessed Jacob—as Jacob. "May he give you and your descendants the blessing given to Abraham" (Gen. 28:1–4). Perhaps this is the blessing Hebrews 11 commends.

Esau's focus was "bless me now." God bountifully blessed both Jacob and Esau during their lifetimes. But much of the blessing of Abraham related to the distant future. God changed Jacob's name to Israel and fulfilled the blessing Isaac spoke over him and his descendants. Thousands of years later, we *see* what Isaac believed by faith. God's promise to bless the world through Abraham's seed was fulfilled in Israel, not Esau. Jesus came from Israel's line.

Jacob and Rebekah's scheming did not secure the blessing for Jacob. It only split the family and brought unnecessary pain. Rebekah never saw her favorite son again.

Jacob's story illustrates the truth of the Scripture: "Do not be deceived: God cannot be mocked. A man reaps what he sows. Whoever sows to please their flesh, from the flesh will reap destruction; whoever sows to please the Spirit, from the Spirit will reap eternal life" (Gal. 6:7–8). The blessing was God's to give. Isaac and Esau couldn't thwart God's plan. Rebekah and Jacob could not hurry it.

God's will sometimes goes against our natural inclinations. When we submit to it, we demonstrate faith that our Father knows best. Such faith opens our eyes to new treasures.

Initially, I said I wouldn't have picked this vignette to showcase Isaac's faith. But like Isaac, I've changed my mind. Isaac reminds us that faith is demonstrated through obedience. Faith supports God's right to choose. He selects heirs to the promise and examples of faith. He defines right and wrong and what's moral and immoral. His blessing is always undeserved.

Are you resisting God's revealed will in an area? Do you think you know better than he does? It's not too late to embrace his revealed will. Doing so landed Isaac in God's hall of faith. What might it do for you?

CLOSING PRAYER

Use this space to turn your insights and responses into prayers.

I Want to Remember . . .

Today's takeaways from #LittleFaithBigGod are:

Day Three

Jacob: Dying with Confidence

Jacob means "he grasps the heel," a Hebrew idiom for "he deceives."

My friend's mother died of breast cancer. Before her death, she told her daughter about a dream she'd had where an irresistible light beckoned her into another world. Every cell in her body yearned to follow the light. But something restrained her.

"My children."

"You'll see them in the twinkling of an eye," the Light promised.

"We'll be together again—soon," she assured my friend when she relayed the dream and grim prognosis.

Whether we are losing a loved one or facing our own demise, death raises concerns. *What will happen to me? What will happen to the people who depend on me?*

In a dream, God showed Jacob a stairway that reached from earth into heaven. Above the stairs, Jacob saw the Lord, who identified himself as "the God of your father Abraham and the God of Isaac." He promised Jacob the blessings he'd given to Abraham.

Jacob's name sounds like the Hebrew words for "heel" or "deceiver." What's so amazing about this awesome revelation is its timing. The Lord delivered this spectacular promise to Jacob while he was fleeing from Esau *after he'd deceived Isaac.* Can you say "grace"? Amazing grace changed this schemer into a new man with a new name.

The transformation wasn't instant, but it was genuine. Today, we'll see his faith sparkle in his final words to his sons.

Scripture Reading..

HEBREWS 11:13, 21

GENESIS 47:28–48:22; 49:28–50:1

Study and Reflection

1. How did Jacob show genuine faith when he was dying?

2. Hindsight bolstered Jacob's faith for the future. Instead of recalling his failures, he recounted God's faithfulness. How might focusing on God's faithfulness help you follow Jacob's example and bless your loved ones (Genesis 48:3–4, 15–16, 21)?

3. How did Jacob prepare his family for his death (Gen. 49:1–2, 28–33)?

4. From Genesis 49:33, what happens to believers after death?

5. What promises do the following Scriptures hold for believers?

a. "But about the resurrection of the dead—have you not read what God said to you, 'I am the God of Abraham, the God of Isaac, and the God of Jacob'? He is not the God of the dead but of the living" (Matt. 22:31–32).

b. "But in the account of the burning bush, even Moses showed that the dead rise, for he calls the Lord 'the God of Abraham, and the God of Isaac, and the God of Jacob.' He is not the God of the dead, but of the living, for to him all are alive" (Luke 20:37–38).

c. "Yes, we are fully confident, and we would rather be away from these earthly bodies, for then we will be at home with the Lord" (2 Cor. 5:8 NLT).

6. In spite of Jacob's stumbles, he finished well. How do you apply this to your life?

7. Even though Joseph was a man of faith, how did he respond when his father died (Gen. 50:1)?

8. Explain the difference faith in Jesus makes when we lose a loved one. "And now, dear brothers and sisters, we want you to know what will happen to the believers who have died so you will not grieve like people who have no hope. For since we believe that Jesus died and was raised to life again, we also

believe that when Jesus returns, God will bring back with him the believers who have died" (1 Thess. 4:13–14 NLT).

The Difference Hope Makes

A few weeks before Christmas, my friend attended the heartbreaking funeral of her twenty-year-old Jewish neighbor. During the ceremony, the rabbi looked at the young man's parents and said, "We are just beginning the happiest time of year [Hanukah], but it will never be happy for you again."

My friend's experience reminded me that without Jesus, death is only bitter.

Another friend's husband died the day after Christmas. The following Christmas, she asked me to decorate her house for the holidays. Hope softened her grief. She knew her husband was with the Lord and she would see him again.

The Promise

Jacob started life grasping his brother's heel. He deceived his father, showed overt favoritism to certain family members, and was passive toward his other children. But, like a maple leaf in autumn, the brilliance of his faith glowed in his last days.

When Jacob wanted to bless his grandsons, Joseph put Jacob's right hand on his older son. Jacob, under the guidance of the Holy Spirit, crossed his hands to give Joseph's second born preeminence. Warren Wiersbe connects the crossing of Jacob's hands to the cross of Christ, reminding us that physical birth doesn't qualify us for heaven. We need a second birth—a spiritual birth (John 3:6–7). "Only the Cross of Jesus Christ can set aside your first birth and establish a second birth."[1]

Jacob had joined Joseph in Egypt seventeen years earlier during a terrible famine. He wasn't even in the Promised Land when he blessed Joseph's sons and promised Joseph a double portion. Jacob worshipped, believing God would fulfill his promise. He instructed his sons to bury him in the land he knew his descendants would one day possess. God's promise was more certain to Jacob than any land deed he could hold in his hand.

"All these people were still living by faith when they died. They did not receive the things promised; they only saw them and welcomed them from a distance, admitting that they were foreigners and strangers on earth" (Heb. 11:13).

God has blessed us with every spiritual blessing in the heavenly realms (Eph. 1:3). Have you taken hold of that promise? Have you passed it on to your loved ones? Is God's promise about a place and a Person you've never seen more valuable to you than what you can see and touch? Do you trust God to lead your family there by grace through faith?

Later generations experienced the blessing Jacob passed on by faith. The hope my friend received from her mother still comforts her decades later. Believing God's promises for the future empowers us to bless others and worship even when we are dying. Faith can make our last days our best days and transform our exit into a spectacular sunset.

CLOSING PRAYER

Use this space to turn your insights and responses into prayers.

I Want to Remember . . .

Today's takeaways from #LittleFaithBigGod are:

Day Four

Joseph: God Will Take Care of You

Joseph means "Jehovah has added."

What is Dying?
by Luther F. Beecher

I am standing upon the seashore. A ship at my side spreads her white sails to the morning breeze, and starts for the blue ocean. She is an object of beauty and strength, and I stand and watch her until she hangs like a speck of white cloud just where the sea and sky come down to meet and mingle with each other. Then someone at my side says: "There! She's gone!" Gone where? Gone from my sight— that is all. She is just as large in mast and hull and spar as she was when she left my side, and just as able to bear her load of living freight to the place of her destination. Her diminished size is in me, and not in her.

And just at the moment when someone at my side says: "There! She's gone!" there are other eyes that are watching for her coming; and other voices ready to take up the glad shout: "There she comes!"

And that is—"dying."[2]

Do you believe God will take care of you when you die? Do you know he will take care of your loved ones after you're gone? To die in peace, we need to know both these assurances.

Two hundred years had passed since God had promised Abraham the land, and Joseph lay dying. The Hebrews still resided in Egypt. "You will leave Egypt and go to the Promised Land. When you go, take my bones," he said. "God will surely take care of you."

Jacob and Joseph believed God would resurrect them and take care of the loved ones they left behind. Joseph had provided for the Israelites while they were in Egypt. He wanted them to know God's care wouldn't die with him. God would continue to provide for Abraham's family long after Abraham, Isaac, Jacob, and Joseph were gone. He would fulfill his promise and bring them into the Promised Land.

Jacob and Joseph peacefully left this earth knowing they'd be reunited with the loved ones who had preceded them in death and later with those they left behind. Until that reunion, God would take care of those on both sides of death. Jesus said, "Whoever lives by believing in me will never die. Do you believe this?" (John 11:26).

Scripture Reading..
HEBREWS 11:22
GENESIS 50:22–25

Study and Reflection

1. Out of a long life of sterling faith, Hebrews chose to highlight Joseph's dying words. Considering what Hebrews 11 has said about faith, what do you think the writer of Hebrews is conveying by underlining this particular scene (Heb. 11:22)?

2. How did Joseph follow his father Jacob's example in Genesis 47:29–30?

3. God's timetable is incalculably bigger than ours. How were Joseph's wishes fulfilled hundreds of years later when the Israelites entered the Promised Land? "And Joseph's bones,

which the Israelites had brought up from Egypt, were buried at Shechem in the tract of land that Jacob bought for a hundred pieces of silver from the sons of Hamor, the father of Shechem. This became the inheritance of Joseph's descendants" (Josh. 24:32)?

4. What do you want to remember from these patriarchs about living, dying, and saying good-bye?

5. Write your own obituary. How do you want to be remembered? What legacy do you want to leave?

Removing the Sting of Death

Screams from the car's backseat jolted author Frank Peretti as he drove his family. A bee buzzed around his allergic son. Gripping the steering wheel with one hand, Peretti snatched the bee with his other. After a moment, he released it.

"Daddy, Daddy, it's still here!" his son cried.

"It can't hurt you anymore," Peretti said, opening his hand to show the stinger embedded in his inflamed flesh. Just as Peretti's hand showed he had taken the bee's stinger, so Jesus's scarred hands and feet show he has taken death's sting.

When I was a child, I asked my mother why we call the day Jesus died "Good Friday." She didn't know. But now I know. It's called *good* because my sins deserved hell, and on the day Jesus died, he took my hell so I could have his heaven. That's good for me!

> Because God's children are human beings—made of
> flesh and blood—the Son also became flesh and blood.
> For only as a human being could he die, and only by
> dying could he break the power of the devil, who had
> the power of death. Only in this way could he set free all
> who have lived their lives as slaves to the fear of dying.
> (Heb. 2:14–15 NLT)

The Apostle Paul wrote,

> When the perishable has been clothed with the imper-
> ishable, and the mortal with immortality, then the
> saying that is written will come true: "Death has been
> swallowed up in victory. Where, O death, is your vic-
> tory? Where, O death, is your sting?" The sting of death
> is sin, and the power of sin is the law. But thanks be to
> God! He gives us the victory through our Lord Jesus
> Christ. (1 Cor. 15:54–57)

I used to think this verse should read, "The sting of death is grief," because that is what we feel when we lose someone. However, the sting in this verse refers to those who die, not to those who mourn.

Strong's concordance says "death" means the death of the body with the implied idea of future misery in hell. *The sting of death is sin.* Those who die in their sins will feel that sting throughout eternity in hell.

But Christ took our sins on the cross (2 Cor. 5:21). He suffered our punishment, so now death for believers is when our mortality will be clothed with immortality. "Then the saying that is written will come true: 'Death has been swallowed up in victory.'"

Christ turned physical death into the gateway to heaven. While on earth, like Joseph who grieved when Jacob died, we grieve the loss of those who've gone ahead. In heaven, we'll do a victory dance and sing, "Thank God! He's given us victory over sin and death through our Lord Jesus Christ."

CLOSING PRAYER

Use this space to turn your insights and responses into prayers.

I Want to Remember . . .

Today's takeaways from #LittleFaithBigGod are:

Day Five
The Gift of Hope

"Soon you will read in the newspaper that I am dead. Don't believe it for a moment. I will be more alive than ever before."
—D. L. Moody

My precious friend Sue Lowe showed her friends and family how to live fully and how to die well. Sue told me to write anything I wanted about her if I thought it could help others. That was Sue.

I've done something better. I asked her daughter, Katie Lowe Garcia, to tell how her mother prepared their family for her parting. Grab a tissue and enjoy Katie's words.

~

I'll never forget the first time my mom had "the talk" with me. I obviously knew she had cancer and hadn't been given a great diagnosis, but up until that point, our focus had really been on how to stay alive—surgery after surgery, treatment and then more treatments, the medical plans and pharmaceutical schedules seemed to somehow make me feel like everything was going to be OK. And if we could just hold on through it all, this would be just a "season" we would *all* look back on as "that time mom had cancer." Even though I knew it wasn't true—I knew the prognosis. I knew where this was headed, and in my heart of hearts, I knew my mom's earthly life was coming to an end. But the illusive feeling of control felt comforting when there was a "treatment plan" in place.

My husband, Steve, and I were visiting my parents, and we had just put the kids to bed. Typically, we all love that time of the evening when we visit. We get the little ones to bed and then we all get something to munch on and spend the next few hours talking and laughing deep into the night. That night, the feeling in the room was different from normal.

"Katie," my mom said. "I'll be dying soon."

The living room was silent.

She talked about how she had struggled with anxiety her whole life; yet she was completely at peace knowing cancer was taking her life. Her famous line, the one we all heard more times than we could count, was "It's either going to be heaven or healing . . . and I win either way."

She was clear and direct and honest about what the doctors were saying and how there really were no more medical options available for her that would be worth pursuing.

I don't remember much more about what she said . . . because I was not OK.

Tears started building up inside of me from depths deeper than I ever knew existed. My face felt hot, and my heart raced. A mixture of anger and devastation spewed out.

"I don't want to talk about this," I yelled through my sobs. "If we talk about this, it means it's actually happening."

Tears streamed down all of our faces.

My mom immediately came and sat on the couch beside me and scooped me into her arms and held me close to her chest. We just sat there. And cried. Together. She rubbed my hair and let me just cry.

After a while, once my breathing started to slow to a normal pace, she looked at me and said, "This is actually happening. And I need us to be able to talk about it. I need to know that you are going to be OK. You need to know that Dad is going to be OK. You need to know that I am OK. I really am."

This night is one I will never forget. That evening, she gave us the gift of honesty. We didn't have to pretend that everything was "going to work out." We didn't have to feel like we had to encourage her to "keep fighting" when we all knew that cancer was going to win. It wasn't a lack of faith—it was reality. And my mom knew that if we could talk about the hard things with her while she was alive, we wouldn't have to be tormented with blanks to fill on our own after she was gone. Secrecy often makes us feel like something is shameful. She gave us the gift to see that death is not shameful. God had redeemed her life, and now God was in the process of redeeming her death, if we would let him.

For the next year, my mom would have this same conversation with anyone who would listen. Neighbors, women in her Bible study, childhood friends, strangers. . . . She made it her life goal to share the goodness of God through a potentially devastating, faith-shattering circumstance. Not a day was wasted. People came to know Christ for the first time because she blessed people with hope as she was dying.

Lessons from Our Experience to Help You

- Sometimes the first conversation is the hardest, so we don't have it. But once that initial conversation is shared, the continued conversations get easier.
- We never told each other how to feel. We knew that each day brought new feelings for each of us. One of us could be feeling sad, while the other was feeling hopeful, or vice versa; but we never tried to talk someone else into feeling how we were in that moment.
- We talked about honest medical facts. We all *know* that God *can* perform a miracle . . . but if we don't face the medical facts, then really we just place ourselves in denial.
- My mom told me over and over again how much she loved me, and why. She reminded me of what I am good at and how those things are going to allow me to live without her. She taught me her cherished recipes; she told me her favorite stories. I wrote them all down.
- We slowed down and just spent time together. Instead of trying to stay busy and "forget" what was happening, we leaned into the reality that death was coming, and so we made each day a memory.

—

I asked Katie to share her experience because it was very different from mine. My parents didn't talk about my mother's pending death. I'm sure they wanted to postpone the terrible grief as long as they could. I already said my family tended to keep emotions light, and losing your mom isn't an airy topic. Maybe since they couldn't figure out how to talk about it without the messy emotions, they dodged the subject. Avoiding the uncomfortable conversation left me wounded. For decades, I felt like I'd failed Mama. We never said good-bye. Did she die feeling isolated and alone? There was a lot I wish we had said to each other.

Don't ignore this topic because it's hard. Prepare your family and yourself. Isaac, Jacob, and Joseph prepared and blessed their children and grandchildren when their lives were drawing to a close. They imparted hope for a future here and in heaven.

Death should not be a taboo subject for those who know Jesus. Letting our loved ones know we know where we're going is a priceless gift. Now, let's taste the hope that awaits all who are in Christ Jesus.

Scripture Reading..
REVELATION 21:1–22:5

Study and Reflection

1. What will Jesus one day do with death? "For he must reign until he has put all his enemies under his feet. The last enemy to be destroyed is death" (1 Cor. 15:25–26).

2. My daughter wanted to spend a year in Europe improving her French after she graduated from university. When she found her dream job in Geneva, Switzerland, I was happy for her but sad she would be an ocean away from me for a year. Death hurts because it means separation. But the Bible's stunning promises offer joy. Here is your opportunity to dream about heaven. List the promises that speak to you from today's Scripture reading. What do you think this

description is trying to convey? If you like, draw a picture and color it. Enjoy reflecting on the hope we have.

3. What have you gleaned from today's discussion to help you with the topic of death?

Gifts of Comfort and Peace

Week after week, Pam attended church—alone. Her husband, Gary, cynically scrutinized her new faith in Christ. She joined the choir, and her church friends prayed with her for Gary. But years passed and nothing happened.

One day while Pam grocery shopped, Gary waited in the parking lot. Sick and tired of his ways, he bowed his head and asked Jesus to forgive him and make him into a new man. But he didn't tell Pam. He wanted to be sure it "took."

One Sunday, while the choir sang and the pastor invited people to the altar to pray, a choir member elbowed Pam and pointed. She stared, not sure she could believe her eyes. Gary strolled toward the altar.

That day, Gary publicly acknowledged his private decision to follow Christ.

God transformed this former skeptic into someone who prayed every morning for those he'd encounter that day. He prayed they might come to know his Savior. His life and destiny flipped 180 degrees.

On December 26, after a brief illness, Gary Lee Pace went home to be with Jesus. His death stunned his family, but his parking lot decision, years earlier, comforted them through their sorrow. Gary was with the Lord, and they would join him one day.

I doubt Gary realized the comfort his faith would bring his loved ones after he died. Have you made that most important decision of asking Christ to be your Savior? Have you let your family know so that when you leave they will have peace and know how to follow in your footsteps?

The apostle John wrote, "I write these things to you who believe in the name of the Son of God so that you may know that you have eternal life" (1 John 5:13). Leaving a will provides practical help for your loved ones, but leaving a testimony provides priceless peace.

CLOSING PRAYER

Use this space to turn your insights and responses into prayers.

I Want to Remember . . .

Today's takeaways from #LittleFaithBigGod are:

Prayer Requests

God Remembered Their Faith, Not Their Flaws

The smell of burning sacrifices made it impossible for Samson to ignore the Philistines' celebration. Samson hung his head. It'd taken blindness and captivity to open his spiritual eyes and loosen the bonds of his self-centeredness. His mother's eyes had shone every time she said, "The Lord himself has chosen you to be his special servant to rescue Israel from the Philistines." How had he not noticed when she stopped reminding him of his calling?

Philistine cheers jolted him from his thoughts. Maybe he could still do something. "O God, please strengthen me just once more," he prayed.

HAVE YOU EVER WONDERED HOW GOD FEELS ABOUT YOU when you've disappointed yourself? Have your setbacks made you question whether God still claims you? My eighty-seven-pound poodle, Max, has helped me with that question.

Max's regal strut has caused grown men to stop their trucks to get a closer look. One time, a bride and groom asked if they could pose for a photo with him.

Whether you've been gone ten minutes or two days, Max's wooly hugs and delighted whimpers say, "Boy, I'm glad you're back."

But Max is also a rascal.

At forty-nine pounds, his eager-to-please half-sister, Cosette, looks up to him literally and figuratively. She plops at the "S" in "Sit." Max, on the other hand, considers whether the treat warrants obedience. He sasses me with high-pitched barks before he reluctantly complies.

"Mom, you know he's cussing at you," my son says.

Like I said, a rascal.

Cosette delights in chasing away squirrels. Using this to his advantage, Max will scratch the door as if he wants to go outside. When I open it, Cosette sprints past in a white blur, expecting Max to follow. But Max steps back and gives me a side-glance. "You dirty dog," I say. His jaw drops into a wolf grin, and he trots over to snatch Cosette's chew.

This week, we'll look at another rascal who doesn't seem to fit in the Hebrews 11 list of those remembered for their faith. We'll also discover others who truly inspire.

Day One
Samson

Samson means "like the sun."

We've already seen that God's family has scamps:

- Abraham lied to a king and said his wife was his sister. This landed Sarah in the king's harem.
- Isaac secretly schemed to give the blessing of Abraham to his favorite son after God had chosen his other son.
- Jacob posed as his older brother in order to steal the blessing.

Today, in my opinion, we look at one of the most challenging examples of all: Samson. He certainly shows that faith, not perfect performance, lights up God's eyes.

God knew some of us would question our worth when we failed. He understood our tendency to trust in what we see instead of in what he says. He knew our flesh would accuse us of never being enough and that we'd feel forgotten when life was hard. So, he recorded stories of real people who stumbled and failed so we could see faith—and grace—in action. He wanted us to know he never forgot them and he will never leave us.

In spite of Max's stubborn streak, I beam when someone asks if he's mine. God claims his characters too. In spite of the flaws of Samson, Jacob, and the rest, the author of Hebrews wrote, "God is not ashamed to be called their God" (Heb. 11:16).

God remembers their faith not their flops. Wow! That means God is cheering our faith—not booing our falls! Let's look at this flawed man that God rescued from an ignoble ending.

Scripture Reading...
Hebrews 11:32
Judges 13:1–15:20

Study and Reflection

Nazirites were not to be near a dead body, eat or drink anything that is produced by the grape vine, or cut their hair (Num. 6:1–8).

1. Read Samson's story in Judges and record your thoughts.

2. Paul wrote, "I urge you to live a life worthy of the calling you have received" (Eph. 4:1). Notice God's participation in Samson's life, as listed below. In light of God's call and involvement with Samson, what expectations might you have for him?

   - The angel of the Lord announced his birth and calling (Judg. 13:2–21).
   - The Lord blessed him (13:24).
   - The Spirit of the Lord began to stir him (13:25).
   - The Spirit of the Lord came upon him, allowing him to tear a lion in two, and gave him supernatural strength against his enemies (14:6, 19; 15:14).
   - God supplied water to quench his thirst (15:19).

What Is Samson Doing Here?

I tore into an envelope addressed to me and pulled out a note with a $200 check tucked inside. The card read, "This is for you—not for your ministry. Buy something you'll enjoy."

My eyes pooled. "Was this a mistake? Why would the Lord have this arrive on this day, when I felt so undeserving?"

Grace. The answer echoed through my mind. Peace washed over me and humbled me.

The day I received the note with the check, I was in the midst of mothering my two small children. We lived on the West Coast while my extended family still lived on the eastern side of the country. Money was tighter than Spanx. We couldn't afford a babysitter for personal time. Hormones and exhaustion had undone me. I didn't even like myself. The timing of this gracious gift unearthed my erroneous view of God. I'd bought the lie that God only blesses the deserving.

That day, the grace of God lifted my weariness. Jesus cared about me, even when I acted ugly. This infusion untapped a fresh reservoir of love I extended to my family.

God showed grace to Abraham when he lied by calling Sarah his sister and when they used Hagar to build a family. He didn't even chastise them. He gently led them forward through their errors.

The Lord blessed Jacob after he conned his father and incensed his brother. Samson also experienced God's grace. God included him smack dab in the middle of a list of some of the most inspiring stories referred to in Hebrews 11. What amazing grace. Tomorrow, we will look deeper into his story.

In her poem "Heaven's Misfits," Ann Luna describes arriving in heaven and being surprised by the people she finds there. As she describes each of the misfits, it dawns on her that these former neighbors and acquaintances are all wondering how she got there!

What a relief; God can spot a heart of faith buried underneath disappointing behavior.

CLOSING PRAYER

Use this space to turn your insights and responses into prayers.

I Want to Remember . . .

Today's takeaways from #LittleFaithBigGod are:

Day Two

Wasted Potential

"God chose things the world considers foolish in order to shame those who think they are wise. And he chose things that are powerless to shame those who are powerful."
—1 Corinthians 1:27 (NLT)

Samson has inspired children for generations. But he wins my vote for least likely to be commended as an example of faith. The book of Judges shows a man driven by sensual and vengeful passions. How did he end up in a chapter on faith?

Samson violated God's moral law and the Nazirite principles God gave to govern him. Yet the Spirit of the Lord used him to rule Israel for twenty years and subdue her enemy, the Philistines. Like the rest of us, Samson was multifaceted. Hebrews 11 reminds us those facets included faith.

If Samson ran for public office today, I think most Christ-followers would resist voting for him. But God chose him to fulfill his purposes in an era when people did what was right in their own eyes. In morally lax societies, godly leaders are as rare as rubies.

Samson's story repeats the cycle found throughout the book of Judges. Israel did evil in the sight of the Lord, so God gave them into the hands of their enemy (Judg. 13:1). This time, God anticipated their need for a deliverer and announced him before his conception.

The angel of the Lord appeared to Samson's mother and said,

> You are barren and childless, but you are going to become pregnant and give birth to a son. Now see to it that you drink no wine or other fermented drink and that you do not eat anything unclean. You will become pregnant and have a son whose head is never to be touched by a razor because the boy is to be a Nazirite, dedicated to God from

the womb. He will take the lead in delivering Israel from
the hands of the Philistines. (Judg. 13:3–5)

What high hopes these words must have raised in Samson's parents.
The Lord had set apart their son from the womb to the tomb to
be his special servant. The angel of the Lord instructed Samson's
mother to practice the Nazirite restrictions her son was to follow.
It's not clear whether this was limited to the duration of her pregnancy, so that nothing unclean would touch Samson, or if she was
to model this lifestyle even after he was born.

There's an important application here. Children are more likely
to imitate our actions than follow our advice. If we tell them not
to lie but make up excuses on why they missed school, which
lesson will they remember? But even modeling right living doesn't
guarantee our children will follow our example. Samson didn't.

Samson's parents appear to be devout followers of Yahweh.
They believed the angel's words. Samson's father, Manoah, prayed
for instructions on how to bring up his son. When the angel of the
Lord appeared, Manoah asked his name, and the angel responded,
"Why do you ask my name? . . . It is too wonderful for you to
understand" (Judg. 13:18 NLT).

The angel of the Lord then ascended to heaven in the flame
of the sacrifice they'd offered. Manoah and his wife fell with their
faces to the ground, thoroughly shaken by the realization that they'd
seen the Lord. Manoah cried, "We are doomed to die." His sensible
wife pointed out she doubted the Lord would have brought this
assignment if he planned to kill them.

Called to Be a Nazirite

A Nazirite was someone who took a vow of consecration to the
Lord. While under the vow, Nazirites would not touch the dead,
eat or drink anything produced by the grapevine, or cut their hair

(Num. 6:1–8). This vow could cover short or long durations. God set Samson and John the Baptist apart as Nazirites for life. They were set apart *to God* from birth (Judg. 13:5).

Nazirite restrictions were to be outward indications of a heart set apart to God. Samson began life adhering to these limits but apparently missed the inner connection to the Lord. Even today, some religious people see holiness mainly as pulling away from the world—focusing on a list of don'ts—instead of drawing near to Jesus. An atmosphere heavy on rules and low on personal engagement is fertile soil for rebels. The purpose of restrictions should be to separate ourselves *from* sin so we can draw near *to* God.

Love fulfills the law of the One who seeks a relationship with us. Joy and kindness mark those who walk by the Spirit, whereas sternness stains the countenance of the self-righteous (Gal. 5:22–23).

The Lord blessed Samson as he grew up and began to stir him (Judg. 13:24–25). But Samson's disappointing actions failed to reflect his calling and nurtured upbringing.

Despite his moral failures, the Spirit of the Lord came upon him at various times, infusing him with supernatural strength. One time, he killed a thousand Philistines wielding only the jawbone of a donkey. Afterward, Samson acknowledged the Lord had provided the victory and cried out to him for water. The Lord caused water to gush out of a hollow in the ground (Judg. 15:18–19). Today, we'll look at the closing chapter of Samson's life and his final hurrah.

Scripture Reading...
JUDGES 13:5; 16:1–31

Study and Reflection

1. What do you learn about the Philistines from these examples?

a. When they couldn't figure out Samson's riddle during his wedding feast, "They said to Samson's wife, 'Coax your husband into explaining the riddle for us, or we will burn you and your father's household to death'" (Judg. 14:15).

b. After Samson burned their fields, "The Philistines went up and burned her [Samson's former Philistine wife] and her father to death" (Judg. 15:6).

2. Read Judges 16:1–22. What does this scene reveal about the persistent and manipulative nature of evil?

3. What warnings and lessons do you take from this passage?

4. Relate the following verses to Samson.

a. "Don't you know that when you offer yourselves to someone as obedient slaves, you are slaves of the one you obey— whether you are slaves to sin, which leads to death, or to obedience, which leads to righteousness?... What benefit did you reap at that time from the things you are now ashamed of? Those things result in death!" (Rom. 6:16, 21).

b. "Do not be misled: 'Bad company corrupts good character'" (1 Cor. 15:33).

c. "Run from anything that stimulates youthful lusts. Instead, pursue righteous living, faithfulness, love, and peace. Enjoy the companionship of those who call on the Lord with pure hearts" (2 Tim. 2:22 NLT).

Identifying Manipulation

A counseling professor once told a woman in one of my husband's lab groups, "Your tears don't move me."

His words stunned the group, but the woman stopped crying. "Those are tears of frustration," he explained, "not brokenness."

I've thought of that many times when someone's tears haven't moved me and wondered what was behind them. Crocodiles shed tears when they eat their prey, but not from regret or sorrow. Some people use tears to manipulate. Others use flattery. If that doesn't work, they nag, pout, or explode to get us to follow their script.

Emotional pain is real. Delilah used it to control Samson, and manipulators use it to control us—if we let them.

One couple I know didn't take a vacation the first twenty years of their marriage. Every time they planned a trip, the mother-in-law became ill and asked, "How can you leave when I'm about to die?"

Pity is another powerful weapon. I once counseled a girl who gave her virginity to a young man at camp. She didn't want to, but she felt sorry for him when he said nobody liked him and she obviously didn't either since she wouldn't sleep with him. She could resist someone she was attracted to because she knew the Scriptures forbade sex outside of marriage. But she couldn't bear this young man's sulking.

Manipulators charm, mope, and threaten to get their way with people. Beware of the intent behind someone's pleas, and never compromise what is right to appease someone or to gain relief from false guilt or weariness.

Giving in to manipulation is not just unpleasant—it destroys. Jesus said no one can serve two masters. Submitting to manipulation makes the wrong person lord over our lives. If Samson had been serving the Lord, he wouldn't have let Delilah or his lusts rule him.

How Do We Protect Ourselves from Manipulation?

Recognizing manipulation is essential to standing against it. The controllers in our lives may be blind to their tactics, but we don't have to be. The closer we walk with Jesus, the better we recognize his voice and the easier it becomes to tune out competing influences. The Bible says we grow in discernment through practice. "But solid food is for the mature, who because of practice have their senses trained to discern good and evil" (Heb. 5:18 NASB).

Giving in to manipulation and tolerating sin keeps us spiritually immature. Samson's callousness to sin made him susceptible to Delilah's schemes.

The ugly feelings we experience when facing manipulation warn us to create healthy boundaries. Consider the following if you suspect you are being manipulated:

- How do I feel after I leave this person or group?
  Feeling weary, selfish, angry, and guilty may indicate someone is trying to control you. I remember when a woman pulled aside a friend of mine, complaining that she had no friends. My friend prayed for the woman but left feeling guilty. On the way home, she experienced an "aha" moment. That woman was a manipulator. My friend's guilty feelings evaporated with this understanding.

Jesus doesn't use guilt, threats, or a victim mentality with us. The fruit of the Spirit displays his character (Gal. 2:22–23).

- What is my motivation? Am I choosing what I believe is the best—or avoiding disappointing or angering someone? In other words, am I avoiding pain or pursuing faith and love?

    Samson didn't tell Delilah his secret because he thought it was the right thing to do. He wanted relief from her pestering. When someone takes more than we want to give, we feel used. Remember, God loves a cheerful giver. Resentful feelings warn us to consider the motive behind our compliance.

    In the long run, caving into controlling people won't protect us from emotional pain. Samson's temporary relief from giving in to Delilah led to greater anguish and loss. We despise our spineless yielding and resent the people we allowed to manipulate us—and anyone who reminds us of them. This isn't love.

    People who habitually let others control them are candidates for self-destructive habits. They mindlessly eat, shop, drink, or gamble to numb the pain of feeling used. Faith is a better motivator than fear, and love is a better inspiration than pity. Jesus never manipulates us. He never shames us. So don't allow others to control you that way either. Godly sorrow over real sin is very different from false guilt.

- Have I counted the long-term cost of compliance?

    When some religious people tried to control a group of believers in the early church, Paul wrote: "It is for freedom that Christ has set us free. Stand firm, then, and do not let yourselves be burdened again by a yoke of slavery" (Gal. 5:1). Standing firm in our God-given freedom may upset those who want to control us. But that isn't bad. Paul also said, "No doubt there have to be differences among you to show which of you have God's approval" (1 Cor. 11:19). Conflict exposes hearts. If one arises because we won't let someone wrongly control us, it's OK. We're in good company.

People with religious-sounding arguments tried to control Jesus, the Apostle Paul, and the disciples. Because these men understood God's will, they escaped their nets by serving one Master, and we can too.

I can't help but wonder how Samson's story would have read if he'd put the Lord first and served him instead of his own base passions. Tomorrow, we will conclude our study of his story.

CLOSING PRAYER

Use this space to turn your insights and responses into prayers.

I Want to Remember . . .

Today's takeaways from #LittleFaithBigGod are:

Day Three
Samson's Weakness

The Holy Spirit came upon people in the Old Testament to anoint them with power and wisdom to accomplish a particular task. In the New Testament, the Holy Spirit indwells believers from the moment we are born into God's family (Eph. 1:13; Rom. 8:9). He promises He'll never leave us (Heb. 13:6). His Spirit empowers us not only to accomplish the tasks God calls us to, but also to live holy lives before him (Eph. 1:19–20).

While we no longer fear losing the Holy Spirit, as Samson did, disobedience grieves God and suppresses his influence and power in us. The Bible tells us to be continually filled with the Holy Spirit (Eph. 5:18). Being filled means submitting to Christ's guidance moment by moment, every day. It's saying, "Thy will be done." It's making Jesus number one in our lives. We can't willfully disobey God and be filled with the Holy Spirit at the same time. Resisting the Lord hurts him and harms us.

Samson's downfall is a physical illustration of the spiritual consequences that await those who repeatedly violate God's laws. His sin deadened his discernment. His enemies used this to capture him, gouge out his eyes, and make him their slave. If we ever wonder if it's OK to play with sin, the memory of blind Samson should jar us to our senses. May we remember his enemies praising their half-man, half-fish idol for his capture while he grinds their grain bound in heavy chains.

Scripture Reading...

JUDGES 16:18–31

Study and Reflection

1. What happened when Samson's sin caught up with him (Judg. 16:18–21)?

2. The Bible notes that the hair on Samson's shaved head began to grow again. Based on Judges 16:28–30 and remembering the call on his life (Judg. 13:5), what else might have been growing besides Samson's hair?

3. From Judges 16:23–31, how does Samson show faith?

4. Samson began with great promise, but he wasted his gifts and special anointing. What do you learn from Samson's story about God?

5. Hebrews named Samson as an example of faith. What do you learn about faith from Samson (Heb. 11:6.)?

6. What personal warnings and applications do you draw from Samson?

A Promising Start, Messy Middle, and Powerful Ending

The Lord endowed Samson with special gifts to lead Israel and deliver her from her enemies. He anointed Samson with superhuman strength and placed him in a nurturing home. He instructed Samson on how to live to protect himself for his calling. Yet Samson squandered his gifts on personal grievances and immoral living. Samson thought he could keep bad company and not get hurt. He paid dearly for his foolishness. Besides the obvious loss of sight and freedom, his defeat made God appear weak and his enemy's idol look strong (Judg. 16:24).

Samson scorned his godly parents' instructions and followed his fallen desires. Instead of humbling himself before God, he let his flesh humiliate him. The Bible says ungodly desires war against us while we live in these earthly bodies. But when we walk by the Holy Spirit, we won't carry out those wrong inclinations (Gal. 5:16). Small acts of obedience add up to big victories and strengthen our godly core. But every time we obey sin, we empower it.

I prove this principle every Christmas season when I add more sweets into my diet. By the beginning of the New Year, sugar is my master. Giving in to my craving strengthens its hold on me.

Samson's downward slide began when he neglected his Nazirite calling. He went into vineyards and feasted for seven days, which easily could have included consuming wine or grapes (Judg. 14:5). He ate honey out of a lion's carcass (14:9) when he wasn't supposed to touch a dead body. He slept with a prostitute. Finally, he gave the secret of his strength to his enemy (16:17–20). He served his lusts instead of the Lord.

While indulging the desires of our flesh increases their hold over us, starving them releases their grip. Colossians 3:5 says, "Put to death, therefore, whatever belongs to your earthly nature: sexual immorality, impurity, lust, evil desires and greed, which is idolatry." "Put to death," means to destroy the strength of or deprive the power of these evil desires. We starve them by considering ourselves dead to sin and alive to God (Rom. 6:11–13).

Bowing to our lusts makes them our masters. In other words, they become idols we serve. We work to satisfy their cravings, be they sensual pleasures or a thirst for security. They control our schedules and sap our energy. The more we serve them, the more they demand from us. They're never satisfied.

Delilah personifies evil. She enticed Samson by pleasing his senses. She begged, cajoled, accused, and nagged to gain his sacred secret. Samson could single-handedly fight off a throng of strong men, but tears were his kryptonite.

The woman who'd pleased his senses now pestered him to death. He thought if he gave in to her unrelenting requests, then he'd have peace and enjoy her again. But sin never plays fair. As soon as Delilah secured his secret, she betrayed him for 1,100 pieces of silver from each of the Philistine lords—knowing they would "afflict" him (Judg. 16:5 NASB).

Satan knows our weak spots. His intent is to steal, kill, and destroy (John 10:10). He's unrelenting. We must be aware of his schemes and our personal weaknesses that he wields against us.

Samson should never have pursued Delilah's company in the first place. He should have fled the first time Delilah used against him what he'd confided. If only Samson had practiced the wisdom of 2 Timothy 2:22: "Run from anything that stimulates youthful lusts. Instead, pursue righteous living, faithfulness, love, and peace. Enjoy the companionship of those who call on the Lord with pure hearts."

Delilah's repeated attempts to trap Samson would have set off an alarm in a healthy person. But Samson had unplugged his God-given radar in order to indulge his desires. In so doing, he surrendered his moral strength. His pride blinded him before the Philistines ever touched his eyes.

In many ways, we share Samson's calling. We were:

- Chosen before we were born. "For he chose us in him before the creation of the world to be holy and blameless in his sight" (Eph. 1:4).
- Equipped to fulfill our calling. "For we are God's hand-iwork, created in Christ Jesus to do good works, which God prepared in advance for us to do" (Eph. 2:10). "God has given each of you a gift from his great variety of spiritual gifts. Use them well to serve one another" (1 Pet. 4:10 NLT).
- Given a spirit of power to accomplish his will for our lives. "For God has not given us a spirit of fear and timidity, but of power, love, and self-discipline" (2 Tim. 1:7 NLT).
- Called to holy living. "I urge you to live a life worthy of the calling you have received" (Eph. 4:1).

If we neglect our calling or squander our gifts on selfish pursuits, then, like Samson, we will suffer great loss. We also will risk missing the joy of hearing our Master say, "Well done."

What sets apart a fallen saint from a scoundrel? Those with true faith will ultimately rise: "For though the righteous fall seven times, they rise again" (Prov. 24:16). Peter and Judas both betrayed Jesus the same night. But Peter returned and led the church. Judas hanged himself.

In Hebrews, God graciously remembered Samson's faith instead of his failures. Samson had time to consider his life while grinding grain for his enemy. God used his defeat to humble him and lift him up for one final victory. Despite all he wasted, Samson believed God rewards those who earnestly seek him, and he died in faith, carrying out the prophetic word concerning him.

God remains constant while our inconsistencies toss us around. His love and faithfulness provide a beacon of hope to guide us home.

His nature cannot change. "If we are faithless, He remains faithful, for He cannot deny himself" (2 Tim. 2:13 NASB).

His love compels him to hate evil (Rom. 12:9). Because he loves us, he hates the sin that destroys us.

Samson's story ends with hope. His great fall awakened his faith. As long as we have breath, even after we've erred, we can return to God and be used for his glory. Hebrews remembers Samson's strength, not his sensuality.

CLOSING PRAYER

Use this space to turn your insights and responses into prayers.

I Want to Remember . . .

Today's takeaways from #LittleFaithBigGod are:

Day Four
A Savior Worth the Suffering

"There were others who were tortured, refusing to be released so that they might gain an even better resurrection."
—Hebrews 11:35

When Larry and I happened upon a lovely museum in Bruges, Belgium, we had no idea we were about to get a moving lesson in history. The paintings depicted saints being martyred. One painting showed men skinning a man in sections while he was still alive. Another showed a believer being drawn and quartered by horses, pulling him in four different directions. These weren't figments of someone's nightmares. They represented historical events involving real people who had names and families. They were people who'd died for their faith rather than renounce it.

After naming many who experienced God's miraculous deliverance—including passing through the Red Sea on dry land and watching the walls of Jericho tumble—the writer of Hebrews turns to others who weren't rescued. He describes them as those "of whom the world was not worthy" (NASB). Even some of those who survived great testing still suffered tremendous loss, including Daniel, Shadrach, Meshach, and Abednego. Hebrews 11 refers to them by experience, not by name.

Although children's Bible stories like to focus on God's amazing rescues, the writer of Hebrews reminds his suffering audience of the patient endurance of those who weren't saved from danger. "But others were tortured, refusing to turn from God in order to be set free. They placed their hope in a better life after the resurrection" (Heb. 11:35 NLT).

Some translations say, "that they might gain an even better resurrection." This may mean they awoke in heaven instead of coming back to life on earth and eventually having to die again. But there could be other reasons why those martyred secured a better resurrection.

Paul told Timothy that the benefits of spiritual disciplines surpass the benefits of physical exercise. While weight training strengthens our physical bodies for a little while, spiritual rigors benefit our souls for eternity. We carry the rewards of a toned faith into heaven. I can't imagine a more intense exercise than willingly enduring torture and death for my faith. I am glad God eternally blesses the martyred.

John saw the martyrs from the Great Tribulation gathered together in a special place: "I saw under the altar the souls of all who had been martyred for the word of God and for being faithful in their testimony" (Rev. 6:9 NLT).

Bible teacher and author Dr. Ken Boa says that God provides a special grace to those called to die for him. He says the spiritual gift of martyrdom is "the ability to display an attitude of joy while suffering or even dying for the faith (1 Corinthians 13:3)."[1] Hebrews 11:35–37 describes some of these heroes.

God will reward all who suffer and die for him in a way far better than we can imagine (1 Cor. 2:9). Some are rewarded in this life. All will be rewarded in eternity. Let's take special note of these individuals, whose faith still shines.

Scripture Reading...
HEBREWS 11:23–40

Study and Reflection

1. Write your observations from today's reading.

2. What lessons and personal applications can you glean?

3. What does this reading teach you about faith?

A Modern Example of Faith and Hope

Athletes often brag after they've won a competition, "I believed in our team. I knew we could do it." Our culture associates *faith* and *hope* with confidence, high fives, and success. Hebrews 11 offers a more sober—and inspiring—take on faith.

Faith in Jesus caused suffering and even death for some of history's finest. But it also provided a hope that carried them through every adversity and into heaven. Trials remind us that we are passing through earth. The time we spend here is a mere blip on the screen of eternity. These witnesses tell us that no matter how brief or long our earthly lives, heaven is our eternal home. Their testimonies have encouraged believers around the world and throughout time who suffer for their faith.

My husband and I once had the privilege to eat lunch with the late Romanian pastor Richard Wurmbrand and his wife, Sabrina. Mrs. Wurmbrand's radiant smile still lights up my mind. I believe her countenance would have glowed in the dark like a full moon at midnight. This is amazing when you consider what they suffered for Jesus.

When the Communists took over Romania, they held a special meeting for pastors, filled with brainwashing and propaganda. Wurmbrand said: "My wife and I were present at this congress. Sabrina told me, 'Richard, stand up and wash away this shame from the face of Christ! They are spitting in his face.' I said to her, 'If I do so, you will lose your husband.' She replied, 'I don't wish to have a coward as a husband.'"

Pastor and Mrs. Wurmbrand were Messianic Jews. They suffered under the Nazis and the Communists. Pastor Wurmbrand spent fourteen years in Communist imprisonment—three of those in solitary confinement, where he saw only his Communist torturers. His body never fully recovered from the torture.

His persecutors drugged his food. They regularly beat him for preaching to fellow prisoners. In his drugged state, the only Scripture he could recall at one point was, "Our Father."

He shrugged, "It was enough. I knew I had a Father."

Sabrina suffered greatly too. The Nazi Party murdered her parents, four siblings, and five children, yet she showed no bitterness or resentment. She continued to show God's love to all. She nurtured the underground church her husband had started and spent three years working in slave labor after being arrested for subversive evangelism.

One of her greatest burdens must have been leaving behind her nine-year-old son Mihai to fend for himself while both of his parents were in prison. Because it was against the law to help families of the imprisoned, the women who did try to help him were beaten so badly they were left crippled.

Our language barrier kept me from talking with Mrs. Wurmbrand, but her countenance communicated more than words. How could she smile after suffering such loss? How could she forgive the years spent in poverty—starving and not knowing if her husband was alive? Her youngest son was a boy when the Communists took his father. He was a man when Richard was finally released.

How did she hold such composure among tragedy? She knew Jesus was worthy of any sacrifice. She "was looking forward to the city with foundations, whose architect and builder is God" (Heb. 11:10).

Finding Faith

None of us knows what trials we'll face. But we know we will be tested (James 1). Someone once said we are either coming out of a trial, in the middle of one, or headed into one. Faith in Jesus prepares us and leads us triumphantly through any challenge. The Scriptures build our faith and equip us for life because they testify about Jesus (John 5:39).

The purpose of Bible study isn't primarily to expand our knowledge. "Knowledge puffs up while love builds up" (1 Cor. 8:1). The purpose is to open our eyes to our glorious Savior. Jesus is the object of biblical faith. Knowing him kindles a hope that won't disappoint. The better we know him, the better we can appreciate those who willingly endured torture for his name.

CLOSING PRAYER

Use this space to turn your insights and responses into prayers.

I Want to Remember . . .

Today's takeaways from #LittleFaithBigGod are:

Day Five
Passing the Baton

"The Christians in Rome were unreasonable," our daughter's high school history teacher ranted. "Rome asked for a small display of respect, but the Christians refused to bow to their deities."

Ginny's teacher sent home historical accounts describing Christians forced to wear bloody animal skins in the coliseum. Crowds cheered as hungry lions tore these early saints apart. I wept as I read these accounts.

In class he mocked these heroes. "Rome gave them what they wanted. They wanted to be with their Jesus."

Our daughter raised her hand and said, "I don't understand. How can you say Rome was reasonable when they killed the Christians?"

"It was a simple thing Rome asked. Like saying the Pledge of Allegiance to the flag."

"I don't understand," Ginny persisted. "How can you say they were reasonable to kill them over a simple thing?"

The cruelty that happened in Rome still happens today. People who hate Jesus behead his followers around the world. Even in our country, they look for ways to squelch our faith.

Children may get a lower grade in school because they don't comply with the lies being taught. Adults may be skipped over for promotions. Is it worth it to stand for Christ?

Yes, yes, yes! If we don't stand in small things, how can we ever hope to stand under real persecution?

Joining Those Who Walk by Faith

Hebrews 11 shows various examples of faith:

- Abel worshipped by faith.
- Enoch walked with God by faith.
- Noah worked by faith.
- Abraham and Sarah received the ability to conceive a son by faith.
- The patriarchs died in faith.
- Others received the ability to be mighty in battle and through weakness were made strong by faith.

God dealt with each person individually. But a common thread wove through their lives. By faith, they obeyed God's guidance. They took him at his word and stood on his promises. They recognized that God was worthy of their total trust and obedience.

You may have heard that you need to find your passion if you want to live a satisfying life. That means discovering a strong motivation or compelling desire that will propel you through the tough parts of life.

But did you know that passion is also related to suffering? Think of the passion of the Christ. "For the joy set before him he endured the cross, scorning its shame, and sat down at the right hand of the throne of God" (Heb. 12:4).

To cultivate commendable faith, we need to live for something and someone bigger than ourselves. Those who know a big God will endure suffering and follow his commands, even when they are unpopular and uncomfortable, just to hear, "Well done, my good and faithful servant."

Sometimes, discovering God's will for our lives is as simple as following the instructions he's already laid out on how to treat people and respond to everyday life. We can't walk in faith and disregard what he says.

Faith in the Routine

The quality of our faith impacts how we treat people. A friend of mine once talked with his buddy who remodels homes about how to have a relationship with Christ. The man said, "You are a fine man, but whenever I walk into a home playing Christian music, I know it won't be a good experience. You are the exception."

My friend understood this man's objections. Those who flaunted their faith often didn't pay on time and expected extra work for nothing. How we treat people says more about our faith than we may realize.

My husband once wanted to tell a woman (who I'll call Jewel) about Jesus. But an inner restraint said, "Not now." He prayed this woman would find the Lord and asked God for the right opportunity.

God heard his prayer and began to show himself to her apart from Larry. One day, Jewel brought up God with Larry.

Jewel volunteers in a local Ronald MacDonald Family Room, which offers a place for family members of seriously ill children to sleep, shower, and launder their clothes. We can imagine the heartbreaking stress and financial strain of its guests.

One woman arrived and handed one of the volunteers five dollars and a coupon. "Would you please bring me a tray of food from the hospital cafeteria?" she said. The volunteer returned and said she was sorry, but they couldn't take the coupon and five dollars wouldn't go far there. The woman pocketed her five bucks and shrugged. She asked to use the shower.

A man in worn clothes who sat reading a book on prayer overheard the exchange. After a bit, he asked Jewel, "How long will she be in the shower?"

"Not long," Jewel said.

But the woman continued to shower for almost an hour. In that time, the man asked again when she'd be out. *He probably wants to give her a religious tract or invite her to his church*, Jewel thought.

Finally, the man approached Jewel a third time. "I have to leave. Please give this to the woman, but don't tell her where it came from." The man held out a roll of bills. "My pastor gave me ninety dollars this morning. I want to give her thirty-five."

"Why would you do that? Your pastor knew you needed this."

"Because that's how God works. He blesses me, so I'll bless others," he said and left.

When Jewel saw Larry, she couldn't wait to relate this story. "God was there! God was there!" she exclaimed.

Larry obeyed the Spirit's nudging to listen instead of to speak. A pastor gave a poor man some cash to help him through the difficult time of missing work to be with his sick child. This man shared more than a third of it with a stranger. And God used it to touch a woman indifferent to Christianity.

A picture really is worth more than words. How might God use our obedience—or disobedience—in ways we'll never know? Let's look at some practical ways to serve Jesus.

Scripture Reading..
HEBREWS 11:39

Study and Reflection

1. According to the following Scripture, what does faith look
    like? "Give thanks in all circumstances; for this is God's will
    for you in Christ Jesus" (1 Thess. 5:18).

2. Why are we able to give thanks even in painful circum-
    stances? "And we know that God causes everything to work
    together for the good of those who love God and are called
    according to his purpose for them" (Rom. 8:28 NLT).

3. Some people are naturally braver than others. Some are
    quicker to show thanks or forgive. But we all need faith to
    function. Read the following Scriptures and consider how to
    apply them. Personalize your application.

    a. Don't conform. "Don't copy the behavior and customs of
        this world, but let God transform you into a new person
        by changing the way you think. Then you will learn to
        know God's will for you, which is good and pleasing and
        perfect" (Rom. 12:2 NLT).

    b. Forgive; don't take revenge. "Do not take revenge, my
        dear friends, but leave room for God's wrath, for it is
        written: 'It is mine to avenge; I will repay,' says the Lord"

(Rom. 12:19). "Be kind and compassionate to one another, forgiving each other, just as in Christ God forgave you" (Eph. 4:32).

c. Pay your debts. "Let no debt remain outstanding, except the continuing debt to love one another, for whoever loves others has fulfilled the law" (Rom. 13:8). "For listen! Hear the cries of the field workers whom you have cheated of their pay. The cries of those who harvest your fields have reached the ears of the Lord of Heaven's Armies" (James 5:4 NLT).

d. Be sexually pure. "God's will is for you to be holy, so stay away from all sexual sin" (1 Thess. 4:3 NLT).

e. Be brave. "For God has not given us a spirit of fear and timidity, but of power, love, and self-discipline" (2 Tim. 1:7 NLT).

f. Trust God in suffering. "Remember, it is better to suffer for doing good, if that is what God wants, than to suffer for doing wrong!" (1 Pet. 3:17 NLT). "So if you are suffering in a manner that pleases God, keep on doing what is right, and trust your lives to the God who created you, for he will never fail you" (1 Pet. 4:19 NLT).

4. What is your main takeaway from studying faith and the lives listed in Hebrews 11?

5. What did you learn about God in our study?

A Practical Faith

I woke up in the middle of the night with knots in my stomach. Two leaks had plunged us into the middle of a major house renovation. Mounting bills and a lack of privacy had taken their toll. Torn-out walls made it possible to look from our master bath through the living room and kitchen to the outside. Our claw-foot tub served as a kitchen sink. My female dog fled upstairs when the first workman arrived and wouldn't reappear until the last one drove away. Larry left for work an hour and a half early and stayed late. Sheetrock dust and mold triggered a chronic cough and breathing issues in me.

Had we heard God right? Was this renovation part of his will? Should we have taken our chances and patched up instead of tearing out?

I opened my Bible to Philippians 4:6–7: "Do not be anxious about anything, but in every situation, by prayer and petition, with thanksgiving, present your requests to God. And the peace of God, which transcends all understanding, will guard your hearts and your minds in Christ Jesus."

As I brought my concerns to God, I remembered the wad of electrical wires our electrician had found under our countertop when we ripped it out. "I can't believe you haven't had a fire," he said. We wouldn't have discovered this hazard if we'd patched the old countertops. We wouldn't have known about the leaky shower with mold hiding behind the sheetrock if we hadn't torn out the back wall. God had not forsaken us. He was protecting us.

I told God that, by his grace, I'd finish this project trusting him. Peace returned. A few days later, a new problem tested my resolve.

After eight weeks of functioning without a kitchen sink and countertop, I couldn't wait to see my finished kitchen. I entered expectantly. In the center of the gleaming white quartzite, two patched chips stood out like snaggled teeth.

I phoned the installers and asked them to reserve another slab. They assured me they'd take care of my concerns.

Their attempt to patch the chips only made them more obvious. When they summoned my husband and me to their shop, I knew we were in trouble. Bottom line—they couldn't get another slab for four months. And there was a good probability the new slab would not match the rest of the kitchen. They were out of options.

I wanted to explode. Hadn't I had asked them to hold an extra slab? But a small voice restrained me. *You promised to trust me with the rest of this project. This is for my glory.*

I realized God had bigger purposes in this project than putting my house back together. Missionaries move to remote areas of the world to share Christ. Would I endure inconvenience for God's glory? Would I represent him to the people he brought into my home?

During the ride to the warehouse, I alternated between praying for a miracle and declaring, "This is for the glory of God." When they showed me their small remnants of quartzite and told me why they couldn't repair my countertop, God showed me a solution. Their eyes brightened; they started measuring. It might work.

A few days later, after it was finally fixed, the man in charge asked if he could hug me. "What could have been our biggest nightmare this year turned out to be one of our best experiences. Thank you."

All I could say was, "Glory to God!"

But our trial didn't end with the countertops. In the upheaval of the remodel, we lost a tiny but necessary part of our cooktop. The appliance man couldn't find a replacement. If we'd known, we'd have cut the tops to fit a new cooktop. We couldn't change the countertops now!

Thinking about tearing out the countertops we'd finally finished overwhelmed me. On top of this, the appliance repairman intimidated me. He complained every time I called. He grumbled as he strode past me, wearing a baseball cap pulled over his eyes with shocks of white hair poking out the back.

I prayed for grace to represent Christ. On his fifth visit, he confided that he used to attend church. "I don't know why my wife and I quit going." When he jimmy rigged a burner to work for Thanksgiving, he praised God! After six trips, our cooktop finally worked.

"I've never seen anything like this," he said. "This has been the worst problem I've dealt with in as long as I can remember. But I feel like a doctor losing a good patient. I hate to say good-bye."

All I could think was, *Glory to God!*

Walking by faith means trusting him in the midst of what we can't control. Not doing so deprives us of peace and denies others a glimpse of Jesus. Who knows the ripple effect of obedient faith?

Faith to Stand Firm

In a good book, all the previous scenes come together at the end. We no longer wonder why the heroine's first love turned out to be a louse. Or why the hero had to lose the promotion to the villain. Something better was awaiting them that could only be realized through those losses.

God's story isn't over. Hebrews 11 ends with a mystery: "yet none of them received what had been promised, since God had planned something better for us so that only together with us would they be made perfect" (Heb. 11:39–40).

Each of us is connected to every saint who's gone before us and to those who will come after us. Our individual stories are paragraphs woven into his grand story. Only when the last page is written will we fully understand the significance of our role in the great story of Christ Jesus. Only then will the dips in God's story make perfect sense. Then faith will give way to sight, and we'll worship our big God.

CLOSING PRAYER

Use this space to turn your insights and responses into prayers.

I Want to Remember . . .

Today's takeaways from #LittleFaithBigGod are:

Prayer Requests

HEBREWS 11

[1]Now faith is confidence in what we hope for and assurance about what we do not see. [2]This is what the ancients were commended for.

[3]By faith we understand that the universe was formed at God's command, so that what is seen was not made out of what was visible.

[4]By faith Abel brought God a better offering than Cain did. By faith he was commended as righteous, when God spoke well of his offerings. And by faith Abel still speaks, even though he is dead.

[5]By faith Enoch was taken from this life, so that he did not experience death: "He could not be found, because God had taken him away." For before he was taken, he was commended as one who pleased God. [6]And without faith it is impossible to please God, because anyone who comes to him must believe that he exists and that he rewards those who earnestly seek him.

[7]By faith Noah, when warned about things not yet seen, in holy fear built an ark to save his family. By his faith he condemned the world and became heir of the righteousness that is in keeping with faith.

[8]By faith Abraham, when called to go to a place he would later receive as his inheritance, obeyed and went, even though he did not know where he was going. [9]By faith he made his home in the promised land like a stranger in a foreign country; he lived in tents, as did Isaac and Jacob, who were heirs with him of the same promise. [10]For he was looking forward to the city with foundations, whose architect and builder is God. [11]And by faith even Sarah, who was past childbearing age, was enabled to bear children because she considered him faithful who had made the promise. [12]And so from this one man, and he as good as dead, came descendants as numerous as the stars in the sky and as countless as the sand on the seashore.

[13]All these people were still living by faith when they died. They did not receive the things promised; they only saw them and welcomed them from a distance, admitting that they were foreigners and strangers on earth. [14]People who say such things show that they are looking for a country of their own. [15]If they had been thinking of the country they had left, they would have had opportunity to return. [16]Instead, they were longing for a better country—a heavenly one. Therefore God is not ashamed to be called their God, for he has prepared a city for them.

[17]By faith Abraham, when God tested him, offered Isaac as a sacrifice. He who had embraced the promises was about to sacrifice his one and only son, [18]even though God had said to him, "It is through Isaac that your offspring will be reckoned." [19]Abraham reasoned that

God could even raise the dead, and so in a manner of speaking he did receive Isaac back from death.

²⁰By faith Isaac blessed Jacob and Esau in regard to their future.

²¹By faith Jacob, when he was dying, blessed each of Joseph's sons, and worshiped as he leaned on the top of his staff.

²²By faith Joseph, when his end was near, spoke about the exodus of the Israelites from Egypt and gave instructions concerning the burial of his bones.

²³By faith Moses' parents hid him for three months after he was born, because they saw he was no ordinary child, and they were not afraid of the king's edict.

²⁴By faith Moses, when he had grown up, refused to be known as the son of Pharaoh's daughter. ²⁵He chose to be mistreated along with the people of God rather than to enjoy the fleeting pleasures of sin. ²⁶He regarded disgrace for the sake of Christ as of greater value than the treasures of Egypt, because he was looking ahead to his reward. ²⁷By faith he left Egypt, not fearing the king's anger; he persevered because he saw him who is invisible. ²⁸By faith he kept the Passover and the application of blood, so that the destroyer of the firstborn would not touch the firstborn of Israel.

²⁹By faith the people passed through the Red Sea as on dry land; but when the Egyptians tried to do so, they were drowned.

³⁰By faith the walls of Jericho fell, after the army had marched around them for seven days.

³¹By faith the prostitute Rahab, because she welcomed the spies, was not killed with those who were disobedient.

³²And what more shall I say? I do not have time to tell about Gideon, Barak, Samson and Jephthah, about David and Samuel and the prophets, ³³who through faith conquered kingdoms, administered justice, and gained what was promised; who shut the mouths of lions, ³⁴quenched the fury of the flames, and escaped the edge of the sword; whose weakness was turned to strength; and who became powerful in battle and routed foreign armies. ³⁵Women received back their dead, raised to life again. There were others who were tortured, refusing to be released so that they might gain an even better resurrection. ³⁶Some faced jeers and flogging, and even chains and imprisonment. ³⁷They were put to death by stoning; they were sawed in two; they were killed by the sword. They went about in sheepskins and goatskins, destitute, persecuted and mistreated—³⁸the world was not worthy of them. They wandered in deserts and mountains, living in caves and in holes in the ground.

³⁹These were all commended for their faith, yet none of them received what had been promised, ⁴⁰since God had planned something better for us so that only together with us would they be made perfect.

Notes

Week One   Acorns and Oaks

[1] Ruth M. Bathauer, *Joy of Living Bible Studies, Hall of Faith: Study on Hebrews 11* (Ventura, CA: Joy of Living Bible Studies, 2005), 14.

[2] R. Kent Hughes, *Hebrews: An Anchor for the Soul* (Wheaton, IL: Crossway, 2015), 296.

[3] C. S. Lewis, *The Silver Chair*. Book 4 of The Chronicles of Narnia (New York: Collier Books, 1970), 134.

[4] Steve Hixon, "A Radical New Identity: Discovering Your Biblical Self-Image," Biblical Resource Ministry of Steve Hixon, http://www.hixonstudies.com/papers/new_identity.asp.

Week Two   Abel

[1] Hughes, *Hebrews*, 296.

[2] John MacArthur, *The MacArthur New Testament Commentary: Hebrews* (Chicago: The Moody Bible Institute, 1983), 301.

[3] Richard Wurmbrand, *Tortured for Christ* (Old Tappan, NJ: Spire Books, 1969), 57.

[4] Neil T. Anderson, *Victory Over the Darkness: Realize the Power of Your Identity in Christ* (Bloomington, MN: Bethany House, 2013), 50, 67.

Week Three   Enoch

[1] Kelly A. Turner, *Radical Remission: Surviving Cancer Against All Odds* (Brilliance Audio, 2014).

[2] Because of his concern about false prophets infiltrating the church of his day, Jude, the brother of Jesus, quoted Enoch's prophecy in the noncanonical book of Enoch (1:9) concerning the future judgment that would fall on the ungodly. The *Ryrie Study Bible* adds this

note: "Though this prophecy is found in the noncanonical book of Enoch (1:9), the original prophecy was uttered by the Enoch of the Bible (Gen. 5:19–24; cf. Heb. 11:5–6) and was later expanded and incorporated in the book of Enoch." Charles Caldwell Ryrie, *The Ryrie Study Bible* (Chicago: Moody Press, 1978), 1892.

[3]Dutch Sheets, *The Pleasure of His Company: A Journey to Intimate Friendship with God* (Minneapolis: Bethany House, 2014), 111.

[4]Anne Graham Lotz, *Pursuing More of Jesus* (Nashville: Thomas Nelson, 2009), 85.

[5]To learn more about confession, see Debbie W. Wilson, *Little Women, Big God* (Abilene, TX: Leafwood Publishers, 2016), chapter 5.

[6]Patsy Clairmont, Barbara Johnson, Marilyn Meberg, Luci Swindoll, Sheila Walsh, and Thelma Wells, *Outrageous Joy* (Grand Rapids, MI: Zondervan, 1999), 65.

[7]J. Vernon McGee, *Thru the Bible with J. Vernon McGee* (Pasadena: Thru the Bible Radio, 1981), 1:37.

[8]Derick Kidner, *Genesis: An Introduction and Commentary,* vol. 1 (Downers Grove, IL: InterVarsity Press, 1967), 89.

[9]William Barclay, *The Letters of John and Jude* (Philadelphia: Westminster Press, 1976), 85.

[10]Anderson, *Victory Over the Darkness*, 48.

[11]"When Americans Become Christians," National Association of Evangelicals, Spring 2015, accessed June 28, 2019, https://www.nae.net/when-americans-become-christians/.

Week Five — Abraham (Part 1)

[1]Randy Alcorn, *The Treasure Principle* (Colorado Springs: Multnomah Books, 2001), 13.

[2]Steven Anderson, "Ur of the Chaldees: Abraham's Original Home," TruthOnlyBible.com, February 13, 2015, https://truthonlybible.com/2015/02/13/ur-of-the-chaldees-abrahams-original-home/.

Week Six — Abraham (Part 2)

[1]To learn more about regret, see Debbie W. Wilson, "You Can Be Freed from Regret," DebbieWWilson.com, July 18, 2017, https://debbiewwilson.com/be-freed-regret/.

Week Seven The Patriarchs

[1]Wiersebe, *Run with the Winners*, 92.

[2]Luther F. Beecher, "What Is Dying?," *Northwestern Christian Advocate*, July 13, 1904, 14.

Week Eight God's Rascals and Heroes

[1]Kenneth Boa, *Conformed to His Image* (Grand Rapids, MI: Zondervan, 2001), 310.

Books.

Blood Brothers

Language of God — Francis Collins

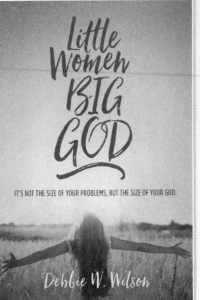